GCSE & 'A REVISI FOR SHAKESPEARE'S *MACBETH*: Scene-by-scene study guide

by Joe Broadfoot

Brief Introduction

This book is aimed at 'A' Level and GCSE students of English Literature who are studying Shakespeare's *Macbeth*. The focus is on what examiners are looking for and here you will find each act and scene covered in detail. I hope this will help you and be a valuable tool in your studies and revision.

Criteria for high marks

Make sure you use appropriate critical language (see glossary of literary terms at the back). You need your argument to be fluent, well-structured and coherent. Stay focused!

Analyse and explore the use of form, structure and the language. Explore how these aspects affect the meaning.

Make connections between texts and look at different interpretations. Explore their strengths and weaknesses. Don't forget to use supporting references to strengthen your argument.

Analyse and explore the context.

Best essay practice

Use PEE for your paragraphs: point/evidence/explain.

Other tips

Make your studies active!

Don't just sit there reading! Never forget to annotate, annotate and annotate!

Introduction

Introduction to Tragedy

According to Aristotle, tragic drama should include both pity and terror which would ultimately lead to **catharsis**. The purpose of tragedy would be best served by a person who is neither completely good nor completely bad morally. In terms of the plot, the ideal would be one whereby the protagonist suffers a reversal in fortune (**peripeteia**) which takes him or her from happiness to misery as a result of some tragic flaw or error (**hamartia**). Along the way, the protagonists should have some moments of insight (**anagnorisis**), when he or she can see exactly how things are.

Tragedy could be subversive even in Elizabethan times. Sir Philip Sidney, for example, said in 1595 that tragedies could 'maketh kings fear to be tyrants'.

Meanwhile, GWF Hegel (1770-1831) claims that tragedy shows what happens when a partial good collides with a partial evil. The audience feel pain watching the destruction of one of these sides or both, but it leads to 'the true ethical Idea '.

Influenced by Hegel, AC Bradley (1851-1935) claimed in 1904 that tragedy emerges from inner conflict and outer conflict. Looking at Macbeth, he wrote: 'treasonous ambition in Macbeth collides with loyalty and patriotism in Macduff and Malcolm: here is the outward conflict. These powers or principles equally collide in the soul of Macbeth himself: here is the inner. And either by itself could make the tragedy '.

Bradley believes that the most deeply felt emotion by an audience watching the tragedy is 'the impression of waste '.

Jonathan Dollimore claims that Elizabethan and Jacobean tragedy could be effective in subverting contemporary gender stereotypes. He says the crisis of confidence in the church and state helped plays to do this.

Like *Richard II*, *Macbeth* questions the rights and privileges of kings and raises the possibility of treason. These were issues that King James I, who ascended the throne in 1603, was very concerned about. He had written *The True Law of Free Monarchies* (1598) about the supreme power of the king, but was aware of the dangers of tyranny, which is why he penned *Basilikon Doron* (1599).

For *Macbeth*, Shakespeare mainly referred to Raphael Holinshed's *Chronicles of England, Scotlande, and Irelande*. Shakespeare used a lot of poetic licence with the character of Banquo, as he was thought to be an ancestor of James I. As not all chroniclers were flattering in their description of Banquo, Shakespeare decided to modify his character and not portray him as a rebel and assassin. In Holinshed, King Duncan is younger and weaker than he appears to be in Macbeth. Once Duncan is murdered, Macbeth rules for 10 years in the historical account. Shakespeare merged this account with the murder of King Duff, who was dispatched by Donwald.

By setting the play in the 11th century, Shakespeare effectively sidestepped censorship, which had resulted in other topical plays being closed down. Treason was a very sensitive subject, especially after the Earl of Gowrie tried to kill King James I while he stayed with him in Perth, Scotland in 1600. Five years later, of course, the Gunpowder Plot, further alerted James I to the dangers of assassination. Henry Garnett, a famous Jesuit, was implicated in this plot. Garnett exercised his right to 'equivocate' when asked to explain himself. This involved misleading questioner by not giving clear answers. This way, Catholics could avoid telling the truth without lying. This was important as many had divided loyalties between England and Rome, the home of their Catholic faith. Garnett's equivocation is more than hinted at in *Macbeth's* porter scene.

Witchcraft was also a very topical subject. King James I was convinced he was the target of daemonic attacks, and he took part in the North Berwick witch trials in 1591. Later, James I composed a book entitled *Demonology* (1597).

Language

The witches speak in a highly stylised, ritualised manner: first they speak in turn and then they deliver a conclusion in unison. These **alliterative choric couplets** are significant in that they introduce **paradox** and **ambiguity** into the play. For instance, 'fair id foul and foul is fair '.

The language throughout is ambiguous. For instance, when the captain describes Macdonwald as 'worthy to be a rebel ', what does that say about Duncan describing Macbeth as a 'worthy gentleman '?

Meanwhile, the **unstable language** in the play mirrors the unstable political situation at the time of the first performances.

There is **dramatic irony** when Duncan says of the previous Thane of Cawdor: 'he was a gentleman on whom I built/an absolute trust '. The irony is increased when Macbeth takes over the mantle of the Thane of Cawdor and also declares his loyalty.

Note that at the time the Scottish Crown did not necessarily the get passed on to the oldest son of the existing monarch. Macbeth shows his irritation with tight **rhyming couplets** after the revelation that Malcolm will succeed Duncan as King.

Context

I've tried to filter out the relevant historical events and only have included those that may have influenced Shakespeare or his play, *Macbeth*.

Shakespeare's life

- born 1564
- aged 18, marries Ann Hathaway
- 1590-4 published works and poems
- 1594 joins Lord Chamberlain's Men
- 1603 renamed the King's Men
- 1599 moves to Globe Theatre

- 1599 - 1608 his 'purple patch': writes *Macbeth*, *King Lear*, *Hamlet* etc
- died 1616

England in 1606

At that time, many believed:

- geocentricism rather than heliocentricism: the sun went round the earth, despite Copernicus's idea that the opposite is the case being proven by Galileo later in 1610
- everything was ordered by God - the monarchy and the church were founded by God
- in witches: James I published the London edition of *Daemonology* in 1603
- in mutability, or change - new stars appeared and disappeared three times in Shakespeare's lifetime - human being must be even frailer and more fragile than the heavens
- the king was God's appointed leader

Government

- Essex executed for treason (like Macbeth, some people considered him too ambitious)
- Queen Elizabeth I died in 1603 and was succeeded by King James I, who was also King James VI of Scotland.
- The succession of King James I to the throne united both kingdoms.

- The union of the crowns was unpopular with many Scots and many English
- In 1603, a law was passed illegalising conjuring up evil spirits and/or grave-robbing
- the Puritans and Catholics arguing in Scotland
- the Gunpowder Plot 1605, an unsuccessful attempt to blow up the Houses of Parliament

Religion

- all children were baptised into the Church of England
- the C of E was under threat from extreme Protestants, Presbyterians and Roman Catholics
- absences from divine services at church could be punishable by fines
- church records kept tabs on the population
- the authorities were alerted to anyone following unusual religious practices, who could be politically dangerous
- approved teaching of religion was received through 'homilies' in parish churches
- the Book of Common prayer was in every church
- the Bible was read aloud in English

Language

- there was very little English literature at the start of the 16th century
- Latin was the language of international scholarship
- translations from Latin resulted in more English words being made and its grammar becoming more flexible

- by the end of the 16th century, English as a language was much more well-developed. Now it was ready for wordplay, especially puns

Drama

- Elizabethans read and translated Roman plays
- all-male acting companies travelled from town to town, setting up in open places or in halls (continuing until the 17th century outside of London)
- In 1576, the Theatre, the first purpose-built playhouse was erected in London
- most of Shakespeare's plays were performed in the Globe
- playhouses were closed in the summer to prevent the spread of diseases, like the plague
- there was censorship of plays, but its severity varied

11th-century Scotland

- families and clans were at war
- each side was led by a thane, and his castle was an important powerbase
- murder and revenge were rife
- the government included the King and a council made up of warlords and church leaders
- communication was difficult because of the landscape

The 'real' Macbeth

- born around 1005
- his family ruled over Moray and Ross
- his father was murdered by his cousins
- he descended from Malcolm the second (Macbeth's grandfather)
- she married Gruach (granddaughter to a high King of Scotland)
- he became Mormaer (great steward) of Moray
- overthrew King Duncan of Strathclyde around 1040. Macbeth thought he had the right to become king through the rules of tanistry (which involved the throne being passed down the mother's line: for instance, the heir or 'tanist' could be the son of the reigning king's sister, instead of the oldest son of the king. Tanistry was later replaced by primogeniture, but in the play, Malcolm's succession is neither tanistry nor primogeniture)

More historical context

The Tiger mentioned by one of the witches could have been a ship that sailed from the Isle of Wight on 5 December 1604 returning after 567 days at sea. That ship was also called *Tiger* and had endured a tempestuous voyage.

Criticism

Terry Eagleton says that the witches 'scorn male power ' by wearing beards. This can be considered positive subversion of is the social hierarchy.

Meanwhile, the critics AC Bradley and G Wilson Knight could be accused of reductionism, as they see much of Macbeth as good versus evil. Similarly, seeing the play as just the conflict between order and disorder may also be too simplistic.

Genre

Like later Gothic novels, the play has a number of doubles, but in the verbal sense as opposed to characterisation. For instance, the captain says 'as cannons overcharged with double cracks,/so they doubly redoubled strokes upon the foe '. This is reminiscent of the witches chant 'double, double, toil and trouble'.

When it comes to gender, Macbeth is not misogynistic describing his wife as 'my dearest partner of greatness '. Lady Macbeth refers to him in more female terms suggesting he is 'to fall of the milk of human kindness '. K. Ryan suggests that this phrase indicates a 'tender nurturing attention to others'. Traditional ideas of both masculinity and femininity are transgressed in the play, particularly by Lady Macbeth who wants to exchange her milk for gall.

Using the semantic field of theology, law and ethics as well as fishing, riding and jumping metaphors Macbeth effectively conveys his intellectual and emotional instability interestingly, Seaton is around as Macbeth and Lady Macbeth come close to their demise. It is almost as if they are descending into hell. This hell was being referred to by the porter, who some consider to be a parody of St Peter. He abandons the place because it's too cold.

Macbeth - simplified version - reported speech

Act 1 Scene 1

In some versions, this is described as an open place, near Forres (about 25 miles from Duncan's royal palace in Inverness). Like all the settings in the play, it is bleak and foreboding, which establishes a Gothic mood and atmosphere.

Some teachers describe the thunder and lightning as 'pathetic fallacy'. I must disagree with that, as the thunder and lightning is not showing a human emotion. However, the weather does effectively set the scene and **foreshadows** the action to come.

The first witch's speech: 'When shall we three meet again / In thunder, lightning, or in rain?' contains an unnatural rhythm of speech and rhyming couplets, signifying the supernatural. She's simply asking when they should meet up next time. Interestingly, she makes it clear that there are only three choices, all involving inclement weather: in thunder, lightning, or in rain.

The second witch's **paradoxical** words in her reply, like 'lost' and 'won' feature a lot in the play, but here the witches gain from any battle, as they will pick up stray body parts for use in potions and other magic. She's simply saying that the next meeting will take place after the battle is over and the noise of it has subsided.

The third witch's use of the **homophone** 'sun' allows the audience to picture the death of a son, i.e. 'the set of sun'. Later in the play, Macduff's son and Siward's son die, so this witch's speech foreshadows what will happen.

The third witch adds that the battle will be over before sunset.

The first witch wants to know where the next meeting will take place. The second witch replies that it should be upon the heath. Once again, the third witch adds extra information, saying that Macbeth will arrive there too. Some teachers link this with the Gothic setting of the moors in Emily Bronte's *Wuthering Heights*. Directors often try to show the audience a bare, untamed, wild place.

After that, spirits call the witches. The first witch is called by Graymalkin, her cat. This is relevant to the **theme** of the supernatural, as witches were said to keep 'familiars' (i.e. spirits inhabiting the body of an animal).The second witch is called by Paddock. This has nothing to do with horseracing! Instead, it is a familiar in the shape of a toad. We don't find out the nature of the third witch's familiar. However, she tells it that she is on the way by saying: 'Anon.'

Before they fly away into the mist, the witches chant in unison: 'Fair is foul, and foul is fair / Hover through the fog and filthy air.' This is **paradoxical**, as how can fair be foul and vice versa?

Act 2 Scene 2

This scene is commonly known as the captain's scene. The captain is sometimes known as, or referred to as, a sergeant; but whatever his rank, he is more often than not portrayed as a valiant soldier. Indeed, it is difficult to foresee the captain being played in any other way. The captain is described by Duncan, the King of Scotland, and Malcolm, the king's son, as 'bloody' and 'hardy' respectively.

Duncan begins by saying, that judging by the captain's appearance, he's certainly been in the wars. Duncan means it quite literally. Therefore, the captain is the right man to ask about the rebellion against the king.

Malcolm confirms description this by saying that the sergeant fought valiantly to save him falling into enemy hands. He directly addresses the soldier, who is on his last legs, or mortally wounded, in many productions.

The captain then tells his story. He begins by saying that it was hard to tell who would win the battle, initially. He compares the two armies to two exhausted swimmers, struggling in the water and hanging onto each other. He adds that although Macdonwald was aided and abetted by soldiers from Ireland and the Hebrides, he was also strengthened by Lady Luck (an imaginary figure presiding over the world and its fortunes). Luck has played a big part. So much so that the captain describes Lady Luck as Macdonwald's prostitute. Macdonwald is so lucky that the captain believes that Lady Luck is metaphorically sleeping with the rebel. It doesn't sound like a loving relationship, as there is a suggestion in the word 'whore' that money has changed hands. Perhaps it is a reference to the mercenaries fighting on Macdonwald's side. It is almost as if Macdonwald has to buy luck as well as mercenaries to fight his corner. Hence, Shakespeare has cleverly manipulated words to make us believe, through the captain's speech, that Macdonwald is tainted by money. The word 'fortune' has a double meaning: luck and money. There is also the **personification** of 'fortune', as it cannot really 'smile', except metaphorically. Therefore, fortune has been invested with human emotions. It and Lady Luck are smiling on the traitor, Macdonwald. Already, the audience will feel that Macdonwald is an unworthy character, who has to buy his victories, friends and lovers.

The simile 'Like valour's minion' describes how Macbeth is like valour's, or bravery's follower. This phrase personifies 'valour', as how can bravery have followers like Macbeth unless it has human qualities? The captain goes on to say that Macbeth was so brave that he laughed in the face of all danger and the misfortune coming his way, and cut a swathe through the ranks all the way to Macdonwald. Once he reached the rebel, Macbeth sliced him from his belly button to his mouth. Finally, he beheaded him and impaled Macdonwald's head upon the stake on top of the castle. Macdonwald meets a grisly end, thanks to Macbeth's bloodthirsty nature. However, this deed is done for Scotland, not for selfish gain.

Duncan's response is to say how brave his first cousin (Macbeth) is, which is understandable as the threat posed by Macdonwald has now been assigned to history. As well as that, Macdonwald's head impaled upon a stick on the castle walls will serve as a reminder to those that rebel against the king.

The captain then tells Duncan and Malcolm that his story is not quite over. He compares what happened next to 'Shipwrecking storms' coming at the beginning of springtime. This describes imaginatively how the Norwegian king mounted a fresh attack upon the captain and his troops. In this part of the speech, this is also clever use of **pathetic fallacy** and a **pun** on the word 'reflection'. The 'sun' could just be shining or it could be reflecting on battles to come, indicated by the 'ship wrecking storms and direful thunders' which **foreshadow** forthcoming action and add extra **Gothic imagery** to the scene.

To this, Duncan asked the question as to whether or not Macbeth and Banquo were frightened by this new onslaught.

The captain's reply was that this new challenge was insignificant to them. To Macbeth and Banquo, they were about as scared as eagles would be if attacked by sparrows, or as a lion would be if attacked by rabbits. Let's not forget that eagles are often compared to kings as they are thought to be the most majestic birds. The same goes for lions, which are kings of the jungle and are also noted for their bravery. Once again, Shakespeare's use of language is a taste of what is to come. In other words, the mention of eagles and a lion **foreshadow** the plot, which sees a new king take the throne. Masculine animal imagery describes Macbeth and Banquo. The 'lion' simile may refer to Macbeth's bravery, while 'eagles' may refer to Banquo's future progeny: a succession of royal birds. There is some dispute over this, with some academics claiming that Macbeth and Banquo were afraid or '[d]ismay'd' by the forces facing them as the captain says 'yes', initially, when asked if they were scared. However, the captain then adds, he means only as much as eagles would be scared by 'sparrows' or a 'lion' would be frightened of a rabbit. The Norwegian king's army is compared to 'sparrows' and a 'hare', animals known for flight rather than fight. There is more evidence to show that Macbeth is the 'lion': later in the play, the third apparition tells Macbeth to be 'lion-mettled' and 'proud'.

The captain continues by saying that they fought twice as hard against the Norwegians, and he likens this to cannons firing twice as many cannonballs as they would normally. He suggests that Macbeth and Banquo wanted to bathe in their enemies' blood. This washing and cleansing imagery is mixed with here with blood, which **foreshadows** what Lady Macbeth does later in the play. The captain also suggests that the carnage was as horrific as Christ's crucifixion at Golgotha. At this point, the captain feels faint and asks for medical attention.

Duncan seems impressed with the captain. The king tells his attendants to take the captain somewhere where he can get medical help, but before that he compares the captain's words to his wounds. It's almost a half pun. Like his words, the captain's wounds bestow honour upon him.

As a captain leaves, Ross (who is portrayed as a war journalist in at least one version of the play) and Angus into the scene.

Duncan appears not to recognise them as he asks his son who it is. Malcolm replies that it is the Thane of Ross, a Scottish nobleman. Interestingly, Malcolm doesn't mention Angus, who has nothing to do with the special beef you can get in McDonald's!

Lennox is the next one to speak and he says that Ross's eyes give him away. He looks stressed. He looks like he has a story to tell.

Ross begins very respectfully by saying: 'God save the King'. Of course, it appears that it is Banquo and Macbeth who have saved King rather than God. Let's not forget Lady Luck was not on the king's side in this battle, according to the captain.

Duncan asks Ross where he's come from. To this, Ross replies he's come from Fife. It seems as if Fife is under the control of Norway, judging by the Norwegian flag flying from a mast that dominates the skyline. He mentions that the Norwegian king had put together an enormous army and was assisted by the disloyal Thane of Cawdor. Macbeth opposed these overwhelming forces, and is described as Bellona's bridegroom. In mythological terms, Bellona is the belligerent wife of Mars, the Roman god of war. It is interesting that Ross compares Macbeth to a woman's 'bridegroom'. Why not simply say that Macbeth was like Mars? It seems to be deliberate on the part of Shakespeare. It may suggest that Macbeth is unduly influenced by his female partner, and that a female force is driving the bloodshed, as we shall see later. The alliteration of the words 'Bellona's bridegroom' gives the meaning even greater emphasis. Ross continues by saying that Macbeth was finally victorious when he broke the enemy's fighting spirit.

Duncan declares how happy he is at this news, to which Ross replies that Sweno, the Norwegian king, now hopes to agree a peace treaty. However, Ross says the Scots would not allow the Norwegians to bury their dead until the enemy had retreated to St Colme's Inch and paid the sum of $10,000.

To this, Duncan replies that the disloyal Thane of Cawdor will never betray him again. He tells Ross to go and announce that the Thane of Cawdor will be executed. The Thane's titles will be taken away from him and given to Macbeth.

Ross says he'll get it done immediately and the scene ends with Duncan saying that the Thane of Cawdor's loss is Macbeth's gain. Of course, this statement is heavy with irony, as Macbeth will become a traitor just like his predecessor as Thane of Cawdor.

Act 1 Scene 3

The three witches appear and it begins with the first witch asking where the second witch has been. The second witch replies she's been killing pigs. The third witch asks the first witch what she's been doing. Prepare yourself for a long answer!

The first witch tells a story of a sailor's wife, a 'rump-fed ronyon' who had chestnuts in her lap. This term was invented by Shakespeare. It refers to a fat female, possibly one with a preference to anal sex, as her 'rump' is well 'fed'. The first witch asked the sailor's wife for one of the chestnuts, but the greedy woman told her to go away. Unfortunately for the food-loving wife, the witch knew where her husband was sailing to. It turns out that the sailor is the master of a ship called the *Tiger*, bound for Aleppo in Syria. The witch threatens to sail to Aleppo in a sieve, which is a kitchen utensil made of perforated metal used the straining. Of course, with all its holes, it's impossible for a conventional sieve to be buoyant in water. The fact that the witch can sail in one demonstrates how powerful she is. When she arrives in Aleppo, she says she will become a tailless rat and perform malicious acts upon the unsuspecting sailor.

The second witch declares that she will offer some assistance to the first witch: providing the wind to help her sail to Aleppo. The first witch approves of this act of kindness, which also shows the power of the supernatural. Not to be outdone, the third witch offers even more wind. You have to wonder whether a Shakespearean pun, or double meaning, is going on at this stage. Perhaps the bawdy bard had flatulent witches in mind for this part of the play.

After the third witch offers more wind, the first witch replies that she already has control of all the winds from every port. She promises she will drain the life out of the sailor. She will prevent him from sleeping for 81 weeks. Once again, you have to wonder what Shakespeare had in mind. Perhaps he was thinking that the first witch would transform herself into a flatulent prostitute in each port and keep the sailor awake every night. He will 'dwindle, peak and pine', perhaps consumed with lust for this witch and the alliterative triplet emphasises her power of him. However, her magic has limitations: she cannot make his ship sink. Nonetheless, she can still conjure up stormy seas. Then, she asks the other witches to look at what she's holding.

The second witch wants to see and she says: 'Show me.' The first witch explains that she is holding a helmsman's severed thumb. Following on from the previous points, it seems that the 'pilot's thumb' is a phallic symbol; it certainly is a severed part taken from another stricken sailor. She adds that this helmsman was drowned while he was returning home.

Suddenly, a drum is heard offstage. The third witch announces Macbeth's arrival. Then all three of them dance in a magic circle, which is necessary for their spell to take effect. It is rather like winding up an old-fashioned clock. If you don't turn the key to wind it up, the clock will not function.

The witches chant in unison that they are weird or, in other words, are supernatural with the power to control fate. Of course, the Fates, or the Parcae in Roman legend, and the Moirae in Greek mythology, were also known as 'the three sisters'. They were so powerful that even the gods were scared of them.

Macbeth and Banquo enter. Echoing the words of the witches, Macbeth says: 'So foul and fair day I have not seen.' In other words, it is a typical day in Britain: the weather is disgusting one minute, pleasant the next. You might say Britain's weather is an oxymoron in itself, but that's another story! Macbeth's speech certainly echoes the witches' speech earlier: 'Fair is foul and foul is fair'. The weather is made all the more significant through the use of **iambic pentamete**r, which makes the language more emphatic.

Banquo asks Macbeth how far it is to Forres, which is on the Moray coast (which sounds a bit like the aforementioned Moirai!) of Scotland. Then he sees the witches and asks what they are. He adds that they look strange and are dressed strangely. He can't believe that they are even from the Earth. He asks if they're alive. He asks if he and Macbeth can ask them questions. He adds that they seem to understand, as each of them has put a finger on their lips, suggesting perhaps that he should remain silent. Banquo remarks that they look like women, but that they have 'beards'. Therefore he's most confused by their masculinity. In the 2010 film, directed by Rupert Goold, the 'beards' are surgical masks.

Macbeth takes over and insists that the witches speak, if they can. He asks them what kind of creatures they are.

The first witch hails him and calls him Thane of Glamis. That's not so surprising, as that is his title. The second witch calls him Thane of Cawdor. That is slightly more surprising to Macbeth, as he has just defeated the Thane of Cawdor in battle. The third witch calls him the future king to add to his surprise.

Banquo notices Macbeth's reaction and he asks him why he looks so startled and afraid. Then Banquo speaks to the witches to find out whether or not they're 'fantastical' illusions. Banquo wonders whether or not the witches are a figment of the imagination. The portrayal of a rational Banquo was flattering to King James I (the monarch when the play was first performed), who was thought to be a descendant. Banquo tells the witches that they've greeted his noble friend and made him speechless with promises of an unlikely but glorious future. He reminds them that they have not said anything to him, personally, yet. However, Banquo makes it clear that he would like to know his future as well. He tells the witches he's not afraid of them.

The first witch simply greets Banquo by saying: 'Hail.' The second witch does the same, as does the third witch. The first witch tells Banquo that he is not as good as Macbeth, yet he is better in some indescribable way. The second witch adds that Banquo is not as happy as Macbeth, yet in some ways he's much happier. The riddles continue as the third witch tells Banquo that his descendants will be kings, although he will not become a king himself. She ends by greeting Macbeth and Banquo once again by saying the word: 'Hail'. The first witch repeats the same greeting.

Macbeth stops the witches, as he fears they're about to leave. He tells them he wants to find out more. He already knows he's the Thane of Glamis, as he inherited the title from his father, Sinel. It can be no coincidence that his father is called Sinel, as it sounds remarkably like the word 'sinner'. It's almost as if Shakespeare is suggesting that Macbeth has bad blood. However, Macbeth is not curious about why he was hailed as the Thane of Glamis. He wants to know how the witches have come to the conclusion that he is also the Thane of Cawdor. Bearing in mind that the Thane of Cawdor is rich and powerful, it seems a tad unlikely or impossible that Macbeth can hold this title too. He wants to know from the witches where they found out about these strange things. It is doubly strange that he is finding out about his future in such a desolate place. He demands that they speak again.

But the witches vanish. Banquo remarks that the Earth has bubbles, and that these witches are similar apparitions. Nevertheless, he is curious as to where they've gone to.

Macbeth surmises that they've vanished into thin air. He wishes they'd stayed, presumably so he could find out more information.

Banquo is questioning his and Macbeth's sanity. He can't believe what they've just seen. He wonders if they've been eating magic mushrooms or some other kind of drugs that cause hallucinations.

Macbeth reminds his friend, Banquo, that his children will be kings. To which, Banquo replies that Macbeth will be a king himself. Macbeth adds that he will also be Thane of Cawdor if he heard right. Banquo says that's exactly what he heard from the witches. Now he wonders who else is approaching, as Ross and Angus enter the scene.

Ross tells Macbeth that the king was happy to hear about his military successes. He adds that his exploits pleased the king so much that he became speechless with pleasure. The king was pleasantly surprised to hear that Macbeth fought against Macdonwald and the King of Norway on the same day. Not only that, Macbeth had no fear of death. Finally, Ross tells him that numerous messages were delivered informing the king of Macbeth's bravery.

Angus adds that the king sent them to say thank you and to bring Macbeth and Banquo back to him. Unfortunately, they are not in a position to pay them.

However, Ross suggests that they can expect reward from the king himself and, as a taster, he begins to call Macbeth, the Thane of Cawdor.

Banquo is particularly shocked. He wonders aloud whether or not the devil can tell the truth.

Even Macbeth is shocked. He asks why they are calling him that when the Thane of Cawdor is still alive.

Angus replies that the man who was the Thane of Cawdor has now been sentenced to death. He adds that he doesn't really know exactly what the former Thane of Cawdor did wrong, but whatever it was it was treasonous, and therefore he has been stripped of his title and is facing death.

Now it's time for one of those famous Shakespearean asides, when the main character reveals something of his true nature. Here, Macbeth talks to himself so only the audience can hear him. He admits the best part of the prediction is yet to come, although he is now pleased to be the Thane of Cawdor as well as the Thane of Glamis. After speaking discreetly to himself and the audience, he thanks Ross and Angus for their good news. He then speaks privately to Banquo asking him whether or not he is beginning to hope that his children will be kings, given that part of the prediction made by the witches is already come true.

Banquo tells Macbeth that if you trust witches, then you may indeed well be on your way to becoming king. However, Banquo says it's strange. He fears it could be a part truth told by the agents of evil to tempt good people to their own destruction. Banquo alludes to the theme of betrayal here, warning Macbeth not to trust the witches, referring to them as 'instruments of darkness'. Then Banquo speaks to Ross and Angus, telling them he would like to have a word with them.

This leaves Macbeth to talk to himself in the audience once again. Macbeth is pleased that the witches have already told him two things that have come true. The alliteration of 'Two truths told' emphasises that Macbeth is morbidly fascinated by the prospect of murdering Duncan to make sure the witches' other prediction comes true. He also thinks it could be inevitable that he will become king as well. He quickly thanks Ross and Angus before continuing to talk to himself. He wonders how such a good thing can be a bad thing, and how a bad thing can be a good thing. Now that his Thane of Cawdor, he is considering murdering King Duncan. To him, the image is horrid, yet he can't help but consider it. The very thought makes his hair stand on end and his heart pound inside his chest. His imagination is more frightening than reality right now. The thought of committing a murder has shook him. So much so that he hardly knows who he is. He's speculating wildly about the future, now he finds it impossible to do anything. Suddenly, the most important things are those that don't exist.

Banquo notices Macbeth's unease and remarks that he is 'rapt', or dazed.

Macbeth is still continuing to talk to himself and the audience. He suggests that if it is fated for him to be king, then perhaps he should just let fate take its course. Perhaps he doesn't have to do anything.

Banquo says to Ross and Angus that Macbeth is not accustomed to these new titles. Like clothes, perhaps they will fit better in time.

Macbeth is still talking to himself in the audience, saying that whatever happens is going to happen. It's a rhyming couplet which makes it seem quite final.

Banquo reminds Macbeth that they are waiting for him. To this, Macbeth says sorry, he was distracted. He tells them that he won't forget how kind they've been to him. Now they should go to the king.

Then Macbeth speaks secretly to Banquo, saying that they have to remember what happened today. After reflecting upon the events, they should talk about it. Banquo agrees. Macbeth says there is no point talking anymore until that moment, and urges all of them to head to the king. So off they go.

Act 1 Scene 4

The scene begins with the sound of trumpets. Feralding the entrance of King Duncan, Lennox, Malcolm Donalbain and their attendants.

Duncan is the first to speak. The king asks if the former Thane of Cawdor has been executed yet. He also asks if those in charge of the execution have returned.

To that, Malcolm replies that they haven't come back yet. However, an insider saw Cawdor die and that same insider said that Cawdor confessed before his execution. Cawdor, apparently, begged for forgiveness and was very honourable in death. He threw away his life as if it were worth almost nothing.

Duncan replies that it's impossible to tell what man is thinking, just by looking at his face. He trusted Cawdor completely. The lines: 'There's no art / To find the mind's construction in the face' are ironic as Duncan cannot read Macbeth's thoughts at all. In fact, Duncan seems to be saying that the impossible task of mind reading is easy, as there's 'no art' to it. It's not something you have to learn, like an artistic skill. Duncan is guilty of underestimating his subjects' ability to scheme, while overestimating his own ability to discover plots against his life. He has learned nothing from the recent rebellion. For James I, this would have been a cautionary tale as, especially after the Gunpowder Plot, he would relate to Duncan's plight.

Interestingly, Macbeth enters just after Duncan has talked about trust. Along with Macbeth, enter Banquo, Ross and Angus. As Macbeth has performed heroics on the battlefield, Duncan is very pleased to see him and addresses him as 'worthiest cousin'. He adds that he was feeling guilty for not having thanked Macbeth enough for saving his realm. He says Macbeth has done so much so quickly that it has been impossible to reward him just as quickly. He says if Macbeth deserved less, then perhaps the reward an offer would have matched the deed. Instead, Macbeth has done more than can ever be repaid.

Macbeth replies that the opportunity to serve his king is reward in itself. He only wants his king to accept what his subjects give him. He explains that it's all about duty: like a son to a father, or servants of a master, so is he bound by duty to his king. He feels duty-bound to do everything he can to keep the king safe, which is ironic given what he plans to do later.

Duncan replies that Macbeth is most welcome. He adds that Macbeth's career will begin to grow in stature now. Then he speaks to Banquo, calling him 'noble'. Duncan says Banquo deserves as much as Macbeth and everyone should know that. Duncan tells Banquo he wants to give him a hug!

You can understand if Banquo was disappointed, but it is a measure of the man that he appears not to be. Perhaps Banquo is of a warmer nature the Macbeth. Being loved may be more important to him than furthering his career prospects. While Duncan is hugging him, Banquo says that 'the harvest' belongs to the king, if he should 'grow'. Cuddles from the king can be seen as quite feminine and motherly, but it shows that Duncan is ready to nurture his subjects like Mother Nature. Banquo recognises this and is offering up his 'harvest', in return. By this, he is referring to how Duncan said he would make Macbeth 'full of growing'. Banquo, clearly, was to grow too. But the fruits of his labours will be given to the king. There is no sign of selfishness in the character Banquo.

Duncan then says how happy he is. He's so happy he has tears in his eyes. He wants his sons, relatives, lords and everyone who knows him to know that he intends to make his eldest son, Malcolm, his successor. (The throne did not necessarily pass from father to son in 11th-century Scotland.) Duncan says his son will now gain the title: Prince of Cumberland. Duncan promises that accolades will shine like stars on everybody else who deserves them, before inviting himself to Macbeth's castle at Inverness. By staying there, Duncan will feel even more in debt to Macbeth, he says.

Macbeth replies that he is accustomed to the kind of physical activity that needs to be done in preparation for the king. Therefore he will race ahead and let his wife know the good news. He says he's going to be the 'harbinger' of the happy news. The phrase 'harbinger of death' comes to mind, as this archaic word for 'a person sent in advance of a royal party or army to obtain lodgings for them' brings with it negative and morbid associations.

Before he goes, Macbeth speaks to the audience in an aside, saying he hopes his plotting does not come to light. Manichaean imagery juxtaposes good versus evil as the battle between 'light' and 'black and deep desires'.

Duncan describes Macbeth as 'worthy'. This is ironic, as Macbeth will prove himself to be 'untrustworthy'. As Macbeth prepares to leave, he talks to himself and the audience in an aside. He says the Malcolm being the Prince of Cumberland is 'a step' which he must jump over. Even that, or he'll fall flat on his face, as Malcolm is now in the Macbeth's way. Macbeth doesn't want the stars to shine light on his dark and terrible desires. It seems as if his eyes are going to be shocked by what his hands do. Obviously, he's talking about murder in a roundabout way. At that point, Macbeth exits.

Blissfully unaware of all of this, Duncan is still talking to Banquo. He's in mid-conversation. He agrees with Banquo, that Macbeth is brave. Duncan has heard so many people praising Macbeth that it must be true. Duncan urges everyone to follow Macbeth, who was gone on ahead to prepare for the royal visit. He adds Macbeth has no equal. The trumpets sound and they all exit.

Act 1 Scene 5

The audience's first exposure to Lady Macbeth is through a **soliloquy**, whereby she reads her husband's letter aloud to herself. It reveals inner thoughts, like Hamlet's 'To be or not to be' soliloquy. This is not to be confused with a **monologue**, whereby a character addresses other characters, as in Henry V's 'Once more unto the breach' speech. She reads her husband's letter aloud which tells the story of how the witches met him on the last day of the battle after his success. It says reliable sources told him they have supernatural knowledge. He tried to question them more but they disappeared. He stood there in shock and next thing him knew messengers from the King arrived calling him the Thane of Cawdor. That was exactly the same title that the weird sisters had called him. They also called him a future king. He thought her should let her know about this, his 'dearest partner of greatness', so she can celebrate too. By using this phrase, Macbeth acknowledges that his wife is at least his equal. He tells her to keep the news secret for now and adds that he'll see her soon.

At this point, she looks up from the letter, and says her husband is the thane of Glamis and Cawdor and he will get what's promised. But she afraid that he is too soft to be an opportunist. He has ambition and wants to be powerful, but lacks the nasty streak he need to be a success. That's **ironic**

foreshadowing, as Macbeth is to prove! Lady Macbeth describes her husband in feminine terms, saying his heart is 'too full o' the milk of human kindness'. It is almost as if she is saying Macbeth has breasts that are full of 'milk', so once again she feminises him.

She adds that Macbeth wants to do everything like a good holy man. He doesn't want to cheat but he want things that are not his. He's afraid to do what he has to do to get those things. She wants him to come home quickly, so she can persuade him. The Fates appear to be on his side, which again is **ironic foreshadowing**. Lady Macbeth seems to have an affinity with spirits: an almost supernatural power. She seems to be the masculine force in this relationship, i.e. 'wearing the trousers' in modern parlance. She is preparing to 'pour spirits' (which could be a pun on alcohol or some other intoxicating liquid) into Macbeth's hole or receptacle, i.e. his 'ear', thus feminising him in metaphorically sexual way. Sigmund Freud might have described this as Lady Macbeth's 'penis envy'. Meanwhile, pouring spirits is another example of **ironic foreshadowing** as she will pour a concoction of alcohol, and possibly drugs, into Duncan's guards' cups to make them fall asleep.

She adds that she'll 'chastise Macbeth with the 'valour' of her tongue. This implies that Lady Macbeth represents 'valour' and, as Macbeth was described earlier as 'valour's minion', he is therefore subservient in this relationship. Yet it could also be argued that she simply conforms to the sharp-tongued wife stereotype.

Then a servant enters and Lady Macbeth asks him or her what's happening. The servant replies the King is coming tonight. Lady Macbeth says it's madness! Macbeth is with the king and why wouldn't he have notified home in advance so she could prepare? The servant apologises but says it is the truth. Macbeth is on the way and sent a messenger on ahead, who has already arrived. That messenger is breathless and exhausted. Lady Macbeth tells the servant to take good care of the messenger as he brings good news.

The servant leaves and Lady Macbeth continues her soliloquy, saying the messenger is short of breath and hoarse like a croaking 'raven'. The raven is personified, as the ill-omened bird is welcoming Duncan to the world of the dead. 'Croaks' is also a **euphemism** for 'dies'. The **iambic pentameter** rhythm of: 'That croaks the fatal entrance of Duncan' makes the line more emphatic.

She tries to conjure up the spirits to give her murderous thoughts and make a less like a woman more like a man. Lady Macbeth seeks to make herself more masculine or at least gender neutral when she says 'unsex me here'. It is almost as if Lady Macbeth want to have a sex change and have her female genitalia sealed up, blocking up her 'passage', preventing physical 'access' to her emotions. Of course, some magical Shakespearean characters are portrayed as androgynous, like Ariel in *The Tempest*, so it could be that Lady Macbeth thinks negating her sexuality will allow her wield more spiritual power.

She wants to be full of cruelty. She wants her blood to thicken so she doesn't feel any remorse. She wants to feel less than human so she can carry out her plans. She asks the spirits to turn the 'milk' in her breasts into acid, poison, bile or 'gall', which could mean she's pregnant or expecting to become pregnant. Interestingly, she's already said that Macbeth is full of a kinder 'milk', so the **juxtaposition** work effectively to show she is the cruellest of the pair.

Lady Macbeth also wants the night to be full of thick smoke so she can carry out murder without the heavens seeing anything untoward. Shakespeare's royal patron, King James I, revealed in his book, *Daemonologie*, that the devil can 'thicken and obscure the air'. Lady Macbeth is invoking help from Hell, so appears to be just as evil as the witches. In the darkness, she adds that her 'keen knife' will not 'see not the wound it makes'. Lady Macbeth's masculinity is revealed here, as she imagines picking up a sharp phallic symbol, i.e. knife and plunging it in. Manichaean imagery highlights the battle between good and evil: the light of 'heaven' versus the 'dark'.

Now Macbeth enters, and his wife hails him as the great Thane of Glamis and the worthy Thane of Cawdor. Lady Macbeth is like a fourth witch, echoing all three witches in Scene 3 when they say: 'All hail, Macbeth'. The third witch adds: 'that shalt be king hereafter!' She adds his letter has taken them into a future that feels already present.

Macbeth replies that Duncan is coming tonight. His wife wants to know when Duncan is leaving. To which, Macbeth replies that it will be tomorrow.

Lady Macbeth says Duncan will never see tomorrow. She adds that Macbeth's face is easy to read like a book, which echoes what Duncan said earlier. She advises her husband to look more welcoming to his king and more like an 'innocent flower'. Nevertheless, he can still be the snake that hides underneath the flower. Lady Macbeth feminises her husband with this simile, suggesting that he portray womanly wiles to his guest while preparing to strike like a snake (a phallic symbol and therefore more masculine). It is also a possible Biblical reference to the serpent in the Garden of Eden, who convinces Adam and Eve to eat from The Tree of Knowledge. This would have resonated with the audience, who were concerned about mutability.

Then she reminds him that the King must be looked after, so she says she'll take care of business for the sake of their joint futures.

Macbeth says they should talk about it more later. His wife replies that he should make himself look more relaxed. If Macbeth looks worried, it will arouse suspicion. She tells him to leave everything else to her. Lady Macbeth is clearly dominant, at this point. Then they exit.

Act 1 Scene 6

Music from an instrument, which sounds like an oboe, plays. The stage is lit by torches. Duncan enters with Malcolm, Donalbain, Banquo, Lennox, Macduff, Ross, Angus and their attendants.

Duncan begins by saying that the castle is a pleasant place, with sweet and which appeals to his gentleness. King Duncan's language is feminine, as he appreciates the fragrant 'air'.

Banquo remarks that it is such a hospitable place that the house martins build their nests on the castle walls. He describes the air as 'delicate'. Banquo speaks in a similar vein to his king, but adds a note of caution, by describing the house martin as 'temple-haunting'. This gives the bird a sense of foreboding, **foreshadowing** the horrors to come. This pleasant exchange outside the castle provides an effective **juxtaposition** with what will happen inside.

Lady Macbeth enters and Duncan calls her 'honoured hostess', which indicates that he is expecting a high level of hospitality and certainly not murder. He says that the love he gets from his subjects can be inconvenient at times, but he still accepts it. Likewise, he's inconveniencing her by being at the castle.

She replies that even if they'd doubled the effort it wouldn't be enough compared to the honours that have been bestowed upon the Macbeth family. It's interesting she uses the word 'double', as earlier featured in the captain's speech about Macbeth's bloody battle and it also featured in the witches' magic spell. The word 'double' is frequently used in the study of Gothic literature, but it has a different meaning here. Lady Macbeth says she's welcoming the king and his entourage as guests.

Duncan asks where's the Thane of Cawdor. They tried to overtake him, and he rode so swiftly that he beat them to the castle. Interestingly, he describes Macbeth's love as 'sharp as his spur'. By the night's end, Duncan will feel exactly how sharp that love is.

Lady Macbeth tells Duncan she and husband are servants to the team and always at his disposal. As well is that, they are ready to give the king back everything that is his.

Duncan asks for her hand, and tells her to bring him to his host, Macbeth. He says he loves him dearly and will continue to bestow honours upon him. They all exit.

Act 1 Scene 7

Like the last scene, hautboys (old-fashioned oboes) are playing and torches are lit.

Then Macbeth says if we're going to do it, then we should get it done quickly. If killing the king would solve all problems, catching them all in a type of fishnet, then he would putting his life and soul at risk just to do it. He reminds himself that there are punishments to consider. Violence breeds violence. What goes around comes around, it seems, as Macbeth discusses the meaning of karma. Already he realises that the witches and his soldiers will betray him, just like he will betray Duncan. Like the soon-to-be murdered King, Macbeth will trust the wrong people. How ironic it is that Macbeth's downfall will be caused by the same untrustworthy behaviour that will topple Duncan. Macbeth is clearly in two minds about continuing with his plan.

Nevertheless, Macbeth is going to allow Duncan to drink from the 'poisoned chalice', or cup. (Interestingly, the England football manager's job is often described as the 'poisoned chalice', as it appears to be a cursed accolade.) Macbeth then mentions the two types of trust involved: 1) he is Duncan subject, so should protect him and 2) he is Duncan's host, so should close the door in the face of any murderers and certainly not assassinate the king! He adds that Duncan has been humble, incorruptible and therefore will be backed by the Angels of heaven who will sing out about the injustice of the killing. Macbeth also personifies Pity, saying it will ride like the wind to spread the awful news. Pity is likened to 'heaven's cherubim', which is a Biblical reference to a cherub. It will ride horses 'of the air', which can be juxtaposed with the witches who 'hover' through the air. However, the wind that is ridden upon will be drowned by tears. Therefore, continuing with the riding metaphors, Macbeth insists that has 'no spur' or motivation to make himself commit this act. All he has is his ambition, which jumps too high for 'intent', or the reason why he's doing this, and crashes down upon it. Macbeth is extremely pessimistic now, and seems ready to give up his plans.

Then Lady Macbeth enters and Macbeth asks her if she has any news. She replies that Duncan has almost finished his dinner. Then she asks Macbeth why he left the dining room.

Macbeth asks her if Duncan has been asking for him. To which, she replies of course he has. Then Macbeth tells that they cannot continue with this plan. He reminds her that the king has honoured him and enhanced his popularity. Macbeth says he enjoys being popular, and he doesn't want throwaway this feeling so quickly.

Lady Macbeth is angry and replies that his 'hope' must've been 'drunk' before. She wonders if his hope 'has' gone to sleep and woken up a greener and paler colour. She says this is a watershed as far as their love is concerned. She questions his bravery. She asks him if he will take the crown that he wants, or whether he will live like a coward instead. She teases him for saying 'I can't' after saying 'I want to'. It reminds her of the proverbial cat who loves fish, but doesn't want to get his paws wet. The feline image further feminises Macbeth.

Macbeth pleads with his wife to be quiet. He says he will only dares to do when a proper man would do. If someone dared to do more, then he would not be a man.

Lady Macbeth is incensed. She replies that if he wasn't a man then what was he when he first mentioned doing this? She says when he dared to do it then he was a man. If he goes one step further by doing what he thought about doing and he will be much more of a man. Before it wasn't the right time or the right place, but he had the guts to consider murder. Now the time and place the right he's having second thoughts. She adds that although she has enjoyed having a baby drinking her milk, she would have slashed its brains out if she had promised to do it, the way as Macbeth has sworn to kill Duncan.

Macbeth asks what will happen if they fail, but Lady Macbeth questions that. She says they can't fail if Macbeth is courageous. While Duncan is asleep, after his long trip to Inverness, she'll get his two servants so drunk that they won't remember anything. While there are asleep, she and Macbeth will be able to do anything to the unguarded Duncan. Whatever they do, all the blame will go on the drunken servants.

Macbeth seems delighted, saying that she should only give birth to male children, as she is so masculine and courageous. He adds that once they have covered the two servants with blood and use their daggers, people will surely believe they are the culprits, won't they?

Lady Macbeth replies that it will be difficult to imagine it happen any other way. Plus, she and Macbeth will make sure they're crying loudly when they find out the news that Duncan has died.

Macbeth tells his decided once and for all to go through with this. He says he will use every muscle in his body to make sure he can commit this awful crime. He tells to go about her business of being a friendly hostess and to hide her 'false heart' with a 'false face'. Then they both exit.

Act 2 Scene 1

Banquo enters with his son, Fleance, who is holding a torch.

Banquo asks his son how the night is going. His son replies that he hasn't heard the clock striking but the moon has disappeared. (Therefore, it appears to be very dark on stage.)

Banquo says the moon usually disappears at midnight. His son respectfully replies that it's probably later than midnight now.

Banquo tells his son to take his sword. He says the heavens are being mean with their light, judging by the darkness all around. He gives him something else too, possibly a shield, before saying he's tired yet he cannot sleep. He's been having nightmares.

Then Macbeth enters with a servant, who is also carrying a lighted torch (not to be confused with a modern-day torch with Duracell batteries!). Banquo hears someone coming and tells his son to give him back the sword. He shouts out 'Who's there?'

Macbeth replies: 'A friend.' Banquo asks him why he's not asleep yet. He reminds him the king's already in bed and in a very good mood to give out presents. He gives Macbeth a diamond which he says is from the king to Macbeth's wife for the incredible hospitality.

Macbeth modestly says anyone prepared for the Kings visit, so couldn't be quite as hospitable as they wanted to be.

Banquo says everything has been alright though. But then he mentions the dreamy had last night about the three witches. He reminds Macbeth that they told him some truth about the future.

Macbeth says he doesn't think about the witches anymore. But he says when they have an hour to spare, they can talk about it again if he wants to.

Banquo says whenever you're ready we can talk about it.

Macbeth tells Banquo that if he stays loyal to him, he will benefit when the time is right.

Banquo says he'll consider it as long as he can keep a clear conscience.

Macbeth tells him to relax for now, and Banquo says the same to you.

At this point, Banquo and Fleance leave. Macbeth now speaks to his servant, telling him to go and tell Lady Macbeth to ring the bell when his drink is ready. Then he tells him to go to bed. The servant duly exists.

Then Macbeth makes one of his most famous **soliloquies**, which begins: 'Is this a dagger I see before me'. It's an imaginary knife conjured up by Macbeth himself or by the witches. In some productions, you can actually see a knife or the image of a knife in front of Macbeth, whereas in others he is simply grasping at thin air. He speaks to the dagger, real or imaginary, saying he wants to hold it. Then he says he can't touch it but he can still see it. Then he wonders if he is hallucinating. Then he compares the imaginary dagger with a physical one he takes out. He then tells the dagger that it 'marshall'st' him, or commands him. This military word suggests diminished responsibility, or a level of insanity.

He says his eyesight must be the one sense that's not working very well. Either that, or it's the only one that's working properly. He says he can still see the imaginary dagger, with blood stains on. Then he says to himself that there is no dagger there. He says murder is making him see one. He says half the world is asleep, enduring nightmares.

Meanwhile, the word 'witchcraft' is personified and the goddess of the moon and sorcery, Hecate (pronounced HEkit, or HEkaTEE: goddess of the moon and sorcery) is invoked. He then personifies 'murder', describing it as being woken up by the howls of the 'wolf', a predator that Macbeth seems to identify with. He continues to describe murder as a person, with it moving as quietly as Tarquin, the last king of Rome who infamously raped Lucretia thus ending the dynasty.

Macbeth then speaks to the ground, telling it not to notice the direction he's walking in. He tells the ground not to echo back and break the silence. Noise could give the game away. He realises that the more he talks, the less courageous he feels. Therefore, he decides to go. He says the murder is as good as done. He can hear the bell, inviting him to do it. He tells Duncan not to hear the bell, because for the king it is a death 'knell' summoning him 'to heaven or to hell'. The final **rhyming couplet** makes those final lines more memorable.

Act 2 Scene 2

Lady Macbeth enters saying that the alcohol that the servants drank has also made her courageous. (Dutch courage, we might call that!) Then she listens carefully. She hears an owl shrieking, and a man ringing the bell. She assumes that Macbeth is now killing the King. The doors to Duncan's bedroom are open, and the drunken servants are making a mockery of their jobs by snoring, when they should be protecting the king. They are so drunk and drugged, that it is almost impossible to tell whether the servants or alive or dead.

Then, off stage, Macbeth calls out, wondering who is there. Lady Macbeth doesn't see him or recognise his voice so she says to herself that she's afraid the servants woke up and the murder didn't happen. She reminds herself that to attempt murder and to not succeed would be the ruin of her and Macbeth. Then she hears a noise. She tells herself she put the daggers where her husband could find them. Surely he couldn't have missed. She says King Duncan reminded her of her own father. If it wasn't for the uncanny resemblance, she might have killed the King herself.

Then Macbeth enters the scene carrying knives splattered with blood. Lady Macbeth sees him and proudly addresses him as 'My husband '.

Macbeth says he's done it and he ask her if she heard anything. She replies that she heard an owl and some crickets. She asked if he said something. Macbeth wants to know when she's talking about. (Notice, at this stage in the play, the speeches between Lady Macbeth become very short. It shows how stressed they are.)

Macbeth asks her who was sleeping in the second bedroom. She replies that it is Donalbain. He then looks down at his bloody hands and calls them 'a sorry sight'. His wife says that's a silly thing to say. Then Macbeth tells her that one of Duncan's sons laughed in his sleep, and one shouted out 'Murder!'. They woke each other up and then they went back to sleep after saying their prayers. We then find out Malcolm and Donalbain are 'lodged together', sharing the 'second chamber'. Macbeth continues by saying that one son cried out: 'God bless us!' While the other said: 'Amen'. He feels as if they saw his murderous hands. He says he couldn't say 'amen' when they said 'God bless us'. At this point, it is obvious that Macbeth feels like he has lost his religion. It is also a sign that Macbeth is bewitched. In contrast, Malcolm and Donalbain are holy, for they are saying their prayers.

Lady Macbeth tells them not to worry about it too much. But Macbeth still wants to know why he couldn't say 'amen'. He says the word stuck in his throat when he had desperate need of God's blessing.

Lady Macbeth says we can't think about it and that if they do they will lose their minds.

Macbeth then says he thought he heard somebody shout out: 'Sleep no more! Macbeth is killing sleep'. He is worried that innocent sleep, that can soothe away all the problems will never visit again.

Lady Macbeth ask him what he's talking about. He continues by saying he kept hearing the words: 'Sleep no more!' It seemed to be addressed to everybody in the house, but it specifically said that Macbeth will sleep no more.

Lady Macbeth asks who said that. She thinks that his strength is weakening. She tells them to get some water to wash the evidence from his hands. She asks him why did he take the daggers out of the room. They were supposed to stay next to Duncan. She tells him to take them back and smear the blood on the guards. Lady Macbeth seems to be suggesting that her 'brainsickly' husband is hysterical, a state traditionally associated with women, with the word 'hysteria' coming from the Greek word for womb, 'hystera'. She suggests that he erase his guilt by washing himself. **Ironically**, she attempts the same thing in vain later in the play.

Macbeth says he can't go back. He's afraid to think about what he's done and can't stand to look at the grisly evidence of it. Lady Macbeth is angry and thinks he is being cowardly. She tells him to give her the daggers. She accuses her husband of being weak calling him: 'Infirm of purpose'. She reminds him that dead and sleeping people are not dangerous and that only children are afraid of them. She says she will put blood on the faces of the servants to make sure they look guilty.

Lady Macbeth leaves and there is the sound of knocking from offstage. Macbeth is worried about whether knocking is coming from. He wonders what's happening to him, as he seems to be frightened of every noise. He looks at his hands and wonders who they belong to. He wonders if all the blood can be washed off by all the water in the oceans: 'Will all great Neptune's ocean wash this blood / Clean from my hand?' He then answers his own **rhetorical question** in the negative, answering 'no'. He thinks the blood will turn their waters red. He finally realises he was right all along to be afraid to commit murder, as he cannot wash away his feelings of guilt.

Lady Macbeth returns and tells her husband that her hands are as red as his now: 'My hands are of your colour'. This is an example of **ironic foreshadowing**, as later she can only see blood on her hands and she is the one trying to wash it off.

However, questioning his courage once more, she says her heart is not as white as husband's. The knocking sound continues in Lady Macbeth says the sound is coming from the south entrance. She says they should go back to their bedroom, but first he should simply wash away the evidence. She is annoyed as he seems to be in shock and unable to do anything.

The knocking continues. Lady Macbeth hears it and says that he should put on his nightgown, in case somebody sees them. She tells him to jump to it and stop being so absorbed in his thoughts.

Macbeth says he wishes he didn't know himself, so he didn't have to think about his crime.

The knocking continues and Macbeth says he wishes it could wake Duncan. He wishes he could undo what he's done. Then he and Lady Macbeth leave the stage.

Act 2 Scene 3

This is often known as the porter scene, which can provide the only comic interlude in a particularly gory play. The porter can be seen as the gatekeeper of the hell which Macbeth has descended into.

The drunken porter enters, and hearing the knocking says there is a lot of it. He says if he were opening the gates to hell he would be turning the key a lot. The knocking continues and the porter pretends he is hell's gatekeeper, by saying: who's there in the devil's name? He wonders if it's a farmer who is killed himself because grain is too cheap. He tells the farmer he's just in time. He tells the imaginary farmer that he should have brought a lot of handkerchiefs with him, as he'll sweat a lot in hell.

The knocking continues and the porter wonders who's there again. This time he thinks it's a treasonous Jesuit, who's not sure if he should follow the Pope or the King. Anyway, he can't fool God, so he'd better come in too. This would have resonated with King James I, who would have no love for Jesuits after the Gunpowder Plot. Jesuit priest Henry Garnett tried to evade the law by 'equivocating' after the plan to blow up the Houses of Parliament had failed. He was executed.

The knocking continues. This time the porter thinks it may be an English tailor, who has used less fabric for people's clothes than he should of, trying to pass them off as tight French fashions. He tells the tailor he will be roasted like a goose. Presumably, this means on a spit.

The knocking continues, and the porter complains he never gets any peace. He says this place is too cold to be Hell, and he doesn't want to pretend to be the devil's porter anymore although he had intended to let people from all professions have the chance to come here.

The knocking continues, and the porter shouts impatiently that he's coming. He tells whoever it is to hold on, and not forget to give him a tip.

The porter then opens the gate for Macduff and Lennox to enter. Macduff appears for the first time, so cannot be implicated in the plot that has ended Duncan's life. Macduff begins by saying to the porter, was it because he went to bed so late that he struggled to get up now?

The porter replies they were drinking until 3 AM and that drink can do three things to a man. Macduff asks what three things are, to which the porter replies, drink can: turn your nose red, put you to sleep, and make you go to the toilet. It can also turn you on sexually, but let you down. It can stimulate your desire, but your performance in bed will suffer. In truth, drink is like a Jesuit, thinking one thing and doing another.

Macduff says it seems as if the porter was under the influence of this lie, last night. The porter admits that the drink got him right in the throat, but he was too strong for it. His legs went a bit wobbly, but he managed to get rid of the alcohol, possibly by vomiting.

Macduff asks the porter if his master is awake yet. At that moment, Macbeth appears on stage, and Macduff says that the knocking must have woken him up.

Lennox greets Macbeth, and the greeting is returned to both of them. Macduff asks Macbeth if the King is awake, to which he replies: 'Not yet.' Macduff says he's been told to wake the king early and already it is later than the time he wanted to get up.

Macbeth says he will take Macduff to Duncan. Macduff says that it is hard work to be a host to the King but it is also an honour. Macbeth says enjoyable work is not really work and points out the door to Duncan's bedroom. Macduff says he'll go and wake the King up and leaves the stage.

Lennox asks Macbeth if the king is leaving today. Macbeth replies that he is and that it has been arranged.

Lennox continues by saying the night has been wild. Wind was blowing down the chimneys; people were hearing cries in the night and strange sounds. There could have even been an earthquake. Strange phenomena was to be expected after the killing of a king. Jacobean audiences believed in a divine order with the king appointed by God; but now this order had been disturbed by Macbeth.

Macbeth agrees that it was a rough night. Lennox says he is too young to remember anything quite like that.

Macduff returns saying he is seen something horrific beyond belief. Macbeth and Lennox simultaneously ask what's wrong.

To which, Macduff replies the worst possible thing has happened. He says it's like murder in a church.

Macbeth is confused, and Lennox wonders if Macduff is talking about the King. Macduff says they should go into the bedroom and see for themselves. He says they will be horrified. He doesn't want to talk about it. They should see it for themselves and then try to put it into words. (This is typical of Gothic literature, in that what has happened is so terrible that it's indescribable.)

Macbeth and Lennox leave the stage to look in the King's bedroom. Meanwhile, Macduff tells everyone to wake up and ring the alarm bell. He calls out Banquo, Donalbain and Malcolm. He tells to shake off sleep, which is a bit like death, and look at the real thing. He tells them to come and witness the horror. He says the bell should ring.

The bell rings and Lady Macbeth enters. She wants to know what's happening and why she can hear the sound of a terrible trumpet, waking everyone up.

Macduff calls her 'gentle'and says this news is not suitable for her ears. He says the news is so bad it would kill her to hear it.

At this moment, Banquo enters and Macduff addresses him telling the king has been killed.

Lady Macbeth reacts in surprise, saying how terrible that is. She asked if it happened in her house.

Banquo says it would be terrible no matter where it happened. He begs Macduff to say that he's lying and that it hasn't happened at all.

Macbeth and Lennox return, and Ross also enters. Macbeth says he wishes he had died an hour before this happened. He says nothing is worth living for now. He says all the wine has gone and there are only the dregs in the bottom left to drink.

Duncan's two sons, Malcolm and Donalbain enter. The latter asks what's wrong. Macbeth says Donalbain's wrong, but he doesn't know it yet. He says the source of their royal blood has come to an end. The images of the 'spring, the head, the fountain' all refer to water, which is associated with blood in this play. They also appear to be references to Duncan's virility, for he is the source from where Donalbain and Malcolm have sprung, i.e. their father.

Macduff puts it more simply by saying their father has been murdered. Malcolm asks who did it.

Lennox says it seems the guards did it as their hands and faces were covered with blood. He adds that their daggers were also covered in blood. He says they looked confused, but they should not have been trusted with the life of the king.

Macbeth says he regrets killing the servants, nonetheless.

Macduff asks why he did that.

Macbeth says it is always possible to be wise after the event when you're calm. He says it was violent rage that caused them to do it. The contrast between the white skinned Duncan and the killers covered in gore caused him to act in haste. Macbeth has cleverly admitted his behaviour has been irrational, but claims it was understandable anger that caused him to kill Duncan's guards. Macbeth uses a rhetorical question to justify his actions: 'Who can be wise, amazed, temperate and furious, / Loyal and neutral, in a moment? No man'. He also could be accused of equivocating, in a way, which is something the porter warned against.

Lady Macbeth suddenly calls for help. The actress playing Lady Macbeth often faints here, which is ironically feminine given her masculine courage in comparison to her husband. She could be manufacturing a distraction, or she could have suddenly realised the enormity of her crimes. Maybe Macbeth needs help more than her, as he is in danger of being found out. Her call distracts Macduff, who tells Macbeth to help his wife.

Malcolm speaks to his brother, Donalbain, in an aside. He asks why they are keeping quiet, when both of them have the most to say.

Donalbain replies that the situation is dangerous and that they should get out. He says they haven't even had time to grieve yet, but they will have plenty of time to do so. Malcolm says the time hasn't yet come for them to turn grief into action.

Like Macduff, Banquo says that someone should look after Lady Macbeth, who goes offstage with her attendants. He adds that when they're properly dressed for the cold weather, they should meet to discuss what can be done. He says they are too shaken to make quick decisions. He says he'll put himself in God's hands, and fight against whatever caused this murder.

Macduff says he will too, as do everybody else on stage. Macbeth says they should get dressed quickly me in the hall. To that, everyone agrees.

Then, all the characters on stage exit, apart from Malcolm and Donalbain. Malcolm asks his brother what he's going to do. He says they should not stay here. He says it's easy for a liar to pretend he feels grief, when he actually feels none at all. He tells Donalbain that he's going to England.

Donalbain says he'll go to Ireland (which seems a bit of a strange place to go, given that some Irish soldiers were involved in the rebellion against his father). He tells Malcolm they will be safer if they go in different directions. He says wherever they go, men will smile at them while holding daggers at the same time. He says they should beware people that are closest to them.

Malcolm says they haven't yet come across that kind of danger, so the best thing to do would be to avoid it. He says they should jump on their horses, and not worry about saying polite goodbyes. And off they ride.

Act 2 Scene 4

Ross enters with an old man, who has the experience to say this is the worst time he can remember in the last 70 years. Ross replies that the old man can see 'the heavens', which must look troubled about what mankind is doing below. The weather is appalling, which suggests that heaven is angry. Although it is daytime, it looks as black as night, with 'dark night' strangling 'the travelling lamp'. Clearly, the lamp that was snuffed out was Duncan, with Macbeth metaphorically plunging Scotland into darkness. This Manichean imagery is used effectively here to emphasise the deplorable state of the nation in black and white terms.

The old man says the weather is as 'unnatural' as the murder of the King. He mentions that last Tuesday a falcon was killed by an owl, that usually only preys on mice. Nature itself has been disrupted by the death of Duncan. This shows the terrible consequences of regicide. King James I could relate to this, as he lived in constant fear of his life.

Ross says something just as strange happened: Duncan's horses escaped. His tame horses seemed to be at war with everyone. The old man says he heard about that. He even heard the horses ate each other.

Ross says he saw it with his own eyes and he couldn't believe it. He tells the old man that Macduff is coming. Macduff duly enters and Ross asked him how things are.

Macduff asks Ross if he cannot see for himself. To this, Ross asked Macduff if anybody knows who committed the murder?

Macduff replies it was the servants, who were killed by Macbeth. Ross says it's a shame that Macbeth did that. He can't understand what would motivate them to do such a thing.

Macduff says they were paid to do it. Malcolm and Donalbain, the king's sons, have fled; so now they are the prime suspects.

Ross complains everything is unnatural. He says how stupid it is that sons can kill the father that supports him. Ross subtly implies that Macbeth may be guilty of Duncan's death, but he is ostensibly talking about Malcolm and Donalbain killing their father. He says Macbeth will probably become king now.

Macduff says Macbeth has already been named king and has gone to Scone to be crowned.

Ross asks Macduff where Duncan's body is. Macduff replies that it is in Colmekill, on the tiny island of Iona in the Hebrides, which is the holy resting place for Scottish kings.

Ross asks if Macduff will also go to Scone, but he replies that he will go to Fife instead. Nevertheless, Ross says he will go on to Scone regardless. Ross seems to look after his own interests primarily. He wants to keep on Macbeth's good side, by travelling to the coronation at Scone.

Macduff wishes Ross well. He says things can't get much worse and hopes 'old robes sit easier' than 'new' ones. This line may tie in with a line later on in the play about Macbeth being too small to wear a giant's kingly clothes. Macduff seems to be suggesting the old king was better suited to run the country than Macbeth.

Ross says goodbye to the old man, who in return blesses him and 'those /
That would make good of bad, and friends of foes'. The latter part of the Old Man's blessing seems to be disapproving of Ross's decision to be loyal to Macbeth, who is a foe.

Then they all leave the stage.

Act 3 Scene 1

Banquo enters and says that Macbeth has everything: he's king, thane of Cawdor and also thane of Glamis, just like the witches predicted. He thinks Macbeth may have cheated to get all of these titles. However, he remembers that Macbeth's descendents will not become kings. Instead, it will be Banquo's descendents that would become kings. He hears a noise, so he is suddenly quiet.

Then a sound of a trumpet is heard, before Macbeth enters, dressed as the King of Scotland. Lady Macbeth enters dressed as his queen. Lennox, Ross, lords, ladies and attendants also enter.

Macbeth notices Banquo and, pointing to him, says he is the most important guest. Lady Macbeth adds that no celebration would be complete without Banquo.

Macbeth speaks to Banquo saying that he wants him to attend the ceremonial banquet that night. Banquo says he will do whatever is commanded.

Macbeth asks Banquo if he's going riding that afternoon. Banquo says he is. Macbeth says he would have liked to have had Banquo's presence at the council meeting that day, but it can wait until tomorrow. He asks if Banquo is intending to ride a long way. Banquo says he'll ride until dinner time and expects to be back an hour or two after sunset.

Macbeth reminds him not to miss the feast and Banquo says he won't.

Macbeth goes on to say that he's heard that the princes have gone to England and Ireland respectively. He adds that they haven't yet confessed to the cruel murder of their own father. Instead, they are telling lies. He tells Banquo they can talk about that and other important things more tomorrow. He tells him to hurry up and get on his horse. He says he'll see him later tonight. He asks him if his son, Fleance is going along with him.

Banquo says he is and it's time for him to go. Macbeth says he hopes that Banquo's horses are fast and not the type to trip up, before saying goodbye. When Banquo leaves.

Macbeth continues speaking. He says everyone can do what they want until seven o'clock tonight. To make society a better place, Macbeth will slink off by himself until suppertime, so he wishes everyone well until then. (He seems to be enjoying playing the role of villain, at this point.) Then, everyone exits except Macbeth and a servant, whom he speaks to. He asks the servant if 'those men' are waiting for him. The servant replies that they are waiting outside the palace gate. Macbeth tells the servant to go and bring them in. So the servant leaves.

We, as an audience, discover Macbeth's inner thoughts as he delivers another soliloquy. In it, he says that it's not much good being the king if you are not safe. He is worried about Banquo. It's Banquo's noble nature that makes him afraid. Banquo is the one person that Macbeth is afraid of. He likens his position to that of Mark Anthony, whose angel feared Octavius Caesar. He reminds himself how Banquo scolded the witches for calling Macbeth king, and how he asked them to tell him his future. That was when Banquo found out he would be the father to a number of kings. Consequently, Macbeth has a crown that he cannot pass on to the member of his family. If this is true, then he's holding 'a barren sceptre'. (This seems to be related to his seeming inability to father a son.) Also, murdering Duncan will mostly benefit Banquo's sons. Macbeth can have no peace of mind now. He has sold his soul to the devil so that Banquo's sons can be kings. Instead of that, Macbeth pledges he will fight Fate, if necessary, to the death. He hears somebody and asks who it is.

The servant returns with two murderers. Macbeth tells the servant to go to the door and stay there until he's called. Once the servant is gone, Macbeth asks the murderers if it wasn't yesterday when they last spoke.

The first murderer says yes it was. So Macbeth continues by asking him what he thought about what was said. Macbeth tells them that Banquo has made their lives a misery for a long time. It wasn't Macbeth, although they thought it was him at the time. He was innocent. He reminds them that he showed them the proof in the last meeting and that he explained how they were deceived. The evidence was so overwhelming that even a halfwit would realise that Banquo was guilty.

The first murderer agrees that everything was revealed in meeting. To which, Macbeth replies that more needs to be done, which is why they are having a second meeting. He asks the murderers if they are so patient that they want Banquo's actions to go unpunished. He asks them if they are so God-fearing that they want to pray for this man who has made them suffer so much.

The first murderer replies that they are simply men. Using bestial imagery, Macbeth agrees that the murderers are part of a species, as much as everything from mongrels to pedigrees can be described as dogs. He adds that if you list the different kinds of dogs according to their qualities, you can tell which ones are fast or slow, which ones are clever or dull-witted, which ones are watchdogs and which ones are hunters. Likewise, Macbeth claims you can classify men. He says if the murderers are not at the very bottom of the list, then they should let him know. If that is the case, he has a plan to get rid of their enemy and make them happy. Macbeth says he'll be sick as long as Banquo is alive. Things will improve once he's dead.

At this, the second murderer speaks up. He says he's been knocked about by the world and has become so angry that he will take any risk to get revenge.

The first murderer agrees. He says he's so sick of the bad luck he's had that he'll take any risk to improve his life.

Macbeth reminds them that Banquo was their enemy, to which they both agree. Macbeth continues by telling them that Banquo is his enemy too. Every moment Banquo is alive affects Macbeth negatively. As king, Macbeth has the power to simply do away with Banquo. However, they have friends in common that Macbeth still needs. That's why he needs the murderers' help. He has to keep the public from knowing about his plans to kill Banquo.

The second murderer tells Macbeth that they will do what he wants them to. The first murderer adds that they are prepared to sacrifice their lives.

Macbeth interrupts them by saying that he can see their fighting spirit shining through. He tells them that within one hour he will let them know exactly where to go and when to strike. He says it must be done tonight and not too near the palace. He reminds them that he must not be suspected. They need to kill both Banquo and his son. He tells them to each make up their own minds about it and that he will come and see them soon.

Both murderers say in unison that they have decided that they are going to do it. Macbeth says he will contact them soon and they should stay inside the palace for now. Then they leave the scene.

Macbeth continues to talk to himself. He says the deal is done and Banquo and his son will be flying to heaven tonight. Then he leaves the scene as well.

(Note that his 'dearest partner of greatness' is not involved in this plot to kill Banquo. Maybe Macbeth has become so paranoid that he cannot even trust his wife. Also, he is trying to change Fate, by killing Banquo's offspring. This is strange as, so far, he's seen all the witches' prophecies come true.)

Act 3 Scene 2

Lady Macbeth enters with a servant. She asks the servant if Banquo has left the court. The servant answers that Banquo has left but he'll be back tonight. She asks the servant to tell her husband that she wants to say a few words to him. The servant agrees to do it and exits.

Lady Macbeth speaks to herself saying if you get what you want and you're still unhappy, then you've spent everything and gained nothing. She thinks it's better to be the victim of a murder, rather than the killer who is racked with guilt.

Mabeth arrives and she speaks to him. She asks him why he's keeping himself to himself. She says sad thoughts should die with the people he was worried about. If he can't sort out the problem, he shouldn't worry about it any more. After all, what's done is done.

Macbeth says they have slashed the snake with a knife, but they haven't killed it yet. The snake will heal itself and be as threatening as before. Both heaven and earth will affected, while meals will be eaten in fear and sleep will be disrupted by nightmares. Macbeth feels he'd be better off dead. Duncan's sound asleep underground and nothing worse can happen to him now.

Lady Macbeth tells her husband to try to look relaxed and happy, as they are entertaining guests tonight.

Macbeth says he will. He hopes his wife can do the same. He tells her to give Banquo special attention and make him feel important. Flattery can do a lot to a lot to hide their murderous intent.

Lady Macbeth tells her husband to stop talking this way, but he says his mind is 'full of scorpions'. In other words, he is suffering great mental anguish while Banquo and Fleance live.

Lady Macbeth says the pair of them won't live forever, but Macbeth says he takes comfort from the fact that they can be killed. That's why she should be cheerful. This dreadful deed will be completed before the bat flies through the castle and the dung beetle sings.

Lady Macbeth asks her husband what he's going to do. Macbeth says she's better off not knowing until after it's done. Then she can clap! He then speaks to the night, almost like a witch, saying keep the day in the dark so the bloody hand is invisible. Then he speaks to himself, saying it's getting dark and the crow is returning to the woods. Gentle creatures are beginning to sleep, while their nocturnal predators are waking up. He speaks to Lady Macbeth next, saying that she seems shocked, but she should not question him yet. The best way to complete bad deeds is to do more bad things. He asks her to accompany him and off they go.

Act 3 Scene 3

The two murderers enter with a third murderer, and the first one wants to know who told the third murderer to join them. The third murderer answers it was Macbeth. (Interestingly, sometimes this role is played by the actor playing Macbeth! In Roman Polanski's film, the third murderer is Ross.)

The second murderer says they shouldn't distrust in the third murderer as they are there for the same purpose.

The first murderer then tells the third murderer to stay with them. He says it's not night yet, and travellers are hurrying to get home or find somewhere to stay the night. Meanwhile, Banquo will be there soon.

The third murderer says he hears horses and then the audience hear Banquo calling from offstage that he need some light. (Ironically, his light is about to be put out.)

The second murderer says it must be Banquo as the rest of Macbeth's guests are inside the palace.

The first murderer says you can hear the horses and the third murderer says it's almost a mile to the palace gate, but

Banquo is likely to leave his horses there and walk the rest of the way to the palace.

Then Banquo and Fleance enter with a torch, which the second murderer sees and mentions to his murderous colleagues. The third murderer identifies Banquo. The first murderer tells the others to get ready.

Banquo then says it's going to rain, and the first murderer interjects by saying: 'Let it come down.' At this point, the murderers attack Banquo, who tells his son to flee. Banquo is killed and Fleance escapes.

The third murderous asks who put the light out. First murderer asks if it wasn't for the best. The third murderer points out that only one person has been killed and the son has escaped. The second murderer says they've failed in the 'best half' of their mission. To which, the first murderer says they should leave and tell Macbeth exactly what they did accomplish.

Act 3 Scene 4

This is often known as the banquet scene. Macbeth , Lady Macbeth, Ross, Lennox, Lords and attendants enter.

Macbeth tells the assembled throng that they know where they should sit, according to rank. From top to bottom, he welcomes all of them. Then they all sit down.

The lords thank Macbeth, who tells them that he will mingle amongst them. Meanwhile, his wife will stay seated until a more suitable time.

Lady Macbeth tells her husband to say 'welcome' to everyone on her behalf.

Then the first murderer appears at the door.

Macbeth continues talking to the guests. He says they are saying thank you to Lady Macbeth. As the table is full on both sides, he will sit in the middle and soon they will propose a toast. Then he goes to the door to meet the murderer, telling him there's blood on his face.

The first murderer says it must be Banquo's. Macbeth is pleased the blood is outside Banquo's body. He asks if Banquo has been killed.

The first murderer tells Macbeth that he cut Banquo's throat himself.

Macbeth compliments the murderer, saying he's the 'best' of the 'cutthroats'. Whoever did the same to Fleance is the best of the best.

The first murderer admits that Fleance has escaped. Macbeth's response is to say that he is having a fit, or a nervous breakdown, again. The news has imprisoned him in fear. He asks again about Banquo.

The first murderer says that Banquo is dead in a ditch with 20 deep gashes in his head. Macbeth thanks him for that. He says the adult snake is dead but the smaller version, or worm, has fled. That worm has no fangs at the moment. He tells the murderer to go and come back tomorrow. The murderer leaves.

Lady Macbeth scolds Macbeth for not entertaining his guests. To that, Macbeth says he's glad that she's reminded him, and he raises a toast to his guests. He says good digestion depends on a good appetite and good health depends on both.

Lennox invites Macbeth to take his seat, but the ghost of Banquo enters and sits in Macbeth's place. Macbeth says that if only Banquo were there all the nobility in Scotland would be under one roof. He says he hopes Banquo's being rudely delayed rather than the victim of something unfortunate.

Ross says that Banquo's absence means that he's broken his promise. Like Lennox, Ross invites Macbeth sit with them.

Macbeth replies and says the table is full. Lennox says there is an empty seat, which has been reserved for Macbeth. As he can't see it, Macbeth asks where it is. Lennox points to where ghost is sitting and then ask Macbeth what's wrong.

Macbeth demands to know who has done it. The lords don't know what he's talking about and then Macbeth talks to the ghost, telling it not to shake its head at him as he didn't do it [commit murder].

Ross tells everyone to stand up because Macbeth is clearly unwell. But Lady Macbeth tells all of them to sit down again, as Macbeth has often been like this since he was a youth. She calls it a 'momentary' fit. She tells them not to pay attention to Macbeth, or they will make his condition worse. Then, in a private aside to a husband, she asks him if he is a man.

Macbeth replies that he is brave, if he dares to look at something that would even scare the devil.

Lady Macbeth says that's nonsense and just one of the hallucinations that he gets when he scared, just like the floating dagger he saw. She says he is like a woman telling a scary story by the fire in front of her grandmother. She says he should be ashamed of himself making silly faces. When he calms down, he will notice is just looking at a stool. (It's an interesting use of language there, as Shakespeare may be saying that Macbeth is looking at excrement and finding more in it than meets the eye. It's a typical sign of madness.)

Macbeth tells he to go over and look for herself. He then speaks to the ghost and asks it what it has to say. He tells it if it can nod then it should speak too. If the dead are going to return like this then there's no point burying anybody. Instead we should let the birds eat our dead. The ghost disappears.

Lady Macbeth asks her husband if he is completely paralysed by his foolish fears. Macbeth replies that he saw the ghost as surely as he is standing before her now.

Lady Macbeth tells him it's shameful nonsense. In response, Macbeth tells her about ancient times when a lot of blood was spilled. He adds that since then, other terrible murders in committed. Before, those murdered used to simply die and that would be the end of it. But now, even a man with 20 fatal head wounds can reappear and knock us off our stools. That's stranger than murder, he says.

Lady Macbeth reminds her husband that his friends are missing him. Macbeth admits he forgot about them. Then he speaks to his guests, telling them not to be alarmed. He says he has a strange mental illness, which is only shocking if you don't know him. He then raises his glass to toast the assembled throng, saying he wants to toast 'love and health to all'. He says he will sit down now and tells them to fill up his cup with wine.

But the ghost of Banquo reappears in Macbeth seat. Macbeth doesn't notice at first, and he says he wants to drink to the happiness of everyone there and to Banquo. He says he wishes Banquo were there. The Lords agree with the toast, and they all drink.

At this point, Macbeth notices the ghost of Banquo. He tells it to get out of his sight and stay in its grave. He says it has no marrow in its bones and its blood is cold. He says it's staring at him with eyes that have no power to see.

Lady Macbeth talks to the guests, who are obviously startled. She's chosen to think of it as nothing more than a strange habit. She says it's nothing more than that, although it does spoil the moment.

Macbeth says he is as brave as any other man. He invites the ghost to come in the form of a Russian bear, or rhinoceros, or an Iranian tiger. He says that would be much less scary. Or he invites the ghost to come back and challenge him to a duel in a deserted place with a sword. If he trembles then, it would be fair to call him a little girl. He tells the horrible shadow to disappear as it's only an hallucination. The ghost vanishes.

Macbeth says he is a man once again, so asks everybody to remain seated. Lady Macbeth says he has ruined the party by making a spectacle of himself.

Macbeth then talks to the guests. He asks them if things like this can happen without making everyone so astonished. He says they make him feel as if he doesn't know himself, when he looks at these terrible things that make him white with fear while they are unaffected.

Ross asks him what things. Lady Macbeth tells them not to speak to him. She says he will only get worse by talking. She advises them to leave immediately, not in rank order, but just to go.

Lennox says good night and wishes the king a speedy recovery. Lady Macbeth wishes them good night too, and everyone leaves except for her and her husband.

Macbeth then says there is an old proverb which says the murdered will get their revenge. Gravestones can move and trees can speak to bring about justice. Crows and magpies have even exposed murderers before. Then he asks his wife what time it is that night.

She replies it's almost morning, but you can't tell if it's day or night. He asks what she thinks about Macduff deciding not to obey the king. Lady Macbeth asks if he actually sent for Macduff.

Macbeth says not exactly, but he will send for him. He explains that he has spies in Macduff's house. He says tomorrow he will go to visit the witches again. He is determined to find out the worst about the future. He says returning to being good would be just as difficult as continuing to kill people. He says he has a few ideas that he wants to put into action before he thinks about them.

Lady Macbeth reminds her husband that he hasn't slept. He says sleep is a good idea. He thinks his delusions may be fuelled by his lack of killing experience. In that sense, they are both just beginners. They both go to bed.

Act 3 Scene 5

There is the sound of thunder as the three witches enter, meeting Hecate.

The first witch ask Hecate what's wrong, as she seems to be angry.

Hecate replies that she has good reason to be livid. She dismissively calls them presumptuous hags. She wants to know why they've given Macbeth riddles and prophecies about his future without consulting her first. She reminds them that she is their controller. To make matters worse, they've done this for a perverse young male, who is unlikely to do anything for them in return. She says they can repair the damage by meeting her at Acheron (which is a Greek mythological name of a river in hell) in the morning. She says Macbeth will go there to find out about his future. She tells them to bring everything with them that they need to make magic. Meanwhile, she'll fly away and work on some horrible spell. She says she has a lot to do before noon, as she has to catch a droplet from the moon, which will help produce magic to trick Macbeth. This magic will fool Macbeth into thinking he is more important than fate itself. He will think he is above everything, and complacency is the greatest enemy of mortal human beings.

Suddenly music is heard, with voices singing: 'Come away'. Hecate says she is being called away by her little spirit, which is sitting in a foggy cloud waiting for her. Then she leaves.

The first witch tells the other two to hurry and leave as well, as Hecate will be back soon. Then they all go.

Act 3 Scene 6

This scene begins with Lennox and another Lord entering. Lennox says that what he said already shows they are on the same wavelength. Strange things have been going on. He says Macbeth pitied Duncan, but that was after he was dead. Banquo was out too late at night, and some may say Fleance killed him as he left the scene of the crime. The moral is not to walk around outside too late at night. And how could Malcolm and Donalbain kill their own father? Lennox notes that Macbeth grieved Duncan's death and killed the drunken servants immediately. That was the right thing to do, wasn't it? It was probably wise too, as it would have been even more outrageous to hear the two of them deny what they had done. All in all, Lennox feels Macbeth has handled a difficult situation well. If only all the murdering sons could be rounded up and put in prison, then they would find out exactly how awful punishment can be, he says. Lennox ends by saying that Macduff is out-of-favour with Macbeth for not to showing up at 'the tyrant's feast'. He asks the Lord where Macduff's hiding.

The Lord responds by saying that Duncan's son, Malcolm, lives in Edward the Confessor's royal court in England. Macduff went there too to ask King Edward for help. He hopes to form an alliance with the Lord of Northumberland, Siward. With their help, Macduff hopes to return peace to Scotland. Meanwhile, Macbeth has heard the news and is so angry that he is preparing for war.

Lennox asks if Macbeth told Macduff to return to Scotland. To this, the Lord replies that he did, but Macduff told the messenger there was no way he would return. The messenger turned his back on Macduff and made him feel that he will regret his decision.

Lennox muses that that may well keep Macduff away from Scotland. However, he believes that someone should tell Macduff to return and free Scotland, which is now under the rule of a tyrant!

The Lord says he will pray for that. Then they both go.

Act 4 Scene 1

The sound of thunder opens the scene and in it we can see a boiling cauldron inside a cavern. The three witches enter.

The first witch says the tawny brown cat has meowed three times, and the second witch says the hedgehog has whined once. The third which says her familiar is telling them to get on with the magic.

The first witch says they should dance around the cauldron and throw in poisoned entrails. She throws in a poisonous toad first. Then the witches chant together: 'Double, double toil and trouble'.

The second witch wants to boil a slice of snake, taken from the fens, or marshes, or bogs. She wants to throw in a lot of other magic ingredients too. The witches chant again.

The third witch wants to add even more unwholesome ingredients, finishing off with a tiger's entrails. They chant in unison once again.

Then the second witch says they'll cool it down with baboon blood. Then it will be finished.

Now Hecate enters along with three other witches and tells them what a good job they've done. She says all of them will share the rewards and she invites them to sing around the cauldron. Music begins to play the six witches sing a song entitled 'Black Spirits'. Hecate leaves.

The second witch says she knows something wicked is coming, as her thumbs are tingling. She says they must open the doors for whoever knocks.

Macbeth enters and ask them what they're doing, describing them as 'secret, black , and midnight hags'. They reply there is no word to describe what they've done. (That's a very Gothic concept: the indescribable.)

Macbeth says he wants some answers to his questions in the name of whoever it is that they serve. He doesn't care about all the terrible things they can do, he just wants to know the answers to his questions.

The first witch tells him to speak. The second witch also. The third witch says they'll answer his questions. Then the first witch asks him if he would rather hear the answers from their mouths or from their masters'. Macbeth says they should call their masters, and then he'll see.

Now the first witch pours the blood of a female pig into the cauldron. And she adds even more ingredients. All the witches chant, telling their masters to show themselves.

There is the sound of thunder and the first apparition is a head wearing a helmet. Macbeth speaks to it, beginning to ask a question. But the first witch says, the apparition can read keep his mind, so Macbeth should just listen and not speak. The first apparition tells Macbeth to beware Macduff, the Thane of Fife. He then asks to go. He descends into the ground or the cauldron.

Macbeth thanks the apparition, saying he guessed as much. He asks for one more word of advice. The first witch says the apparition will not be commanded. However, another one is coming who is stronger than the first.

We hear thunder again, and a second apparition appears which looks like a bloody child. It calls out Macbeth's name three times, to which he replies that he would listen with all three ears if he had them.

The second apparition continues by telling Macbeth to be strong. He can laugh at the power of other men, has nobody born from a woman can ever hope to hurt him. The second apparition also descends.

Macbeth concludes that he doesn't need to kill Macduff and has no reason to feel afraid of him. Nonetheless, he wants to make doubly sure by killing Macduff. At least then he can sleep better at night.

The sound of thunder is heard again, and the third apparition appears. This one looks like a child with a crown on its head. It is holding a tree in its hand. Macbeth asks what it is.

All the witches tell him to listen but not speak to it. The third apparition tells Macbeth to be brave like a lion and proud. It tells him not to worry about who is conspiring against him. It tells him he will never be defeated until Birnam Wood marches to fight him at Dunsinane Hill. Then it descends.

Macbeth says that will never happen. How can the trees pull their roots out of the earth and march? He considers what the apparitions have said to be good omens. But he wants to ask one more question: will Banquo's sons ever reign in Scotland.

The witches tell him not to ask any more. Macbeth says if they don't answer then he will curse them. He asks why the cauldron sinking and what the noise is.

The music of hautboys is heard. Each of the three original witches says: 'Show'. Then, they all chant in unison: 'Show his eyes and grieve his heart'. Eight kings march across the stage, with the last one holding the mirror. They are followed by Banquo.

Macbeth says that spirit looks too much like the ghost of Banquo. He tells it to go away. He asks the witches why they are showing him this. In the mirror he can see many more men. Some of these future kings are kings of more than one country. And to make it even worse, Banquo is smiling and pointing at them. He asks if this is a true prophecy.

The first witch says it's true, but there's no point in Macbeth looking so confused. She then tells her sisters to try to cheer Macbeth up by dancing and showing him 'the best' of their 'delights'. Music plays, they dance and then they vanish.

Macbeth wonders where they've gone. He says this hour will be marked in the calendar as cursed. He calls to somebody off stage to come in and Lennox enters.

Lennox asks Macbeth what he wants. In reply, Macbeth asks Lennox if he saw the witches. Lennox says he didn't. Macbeth ask Lennox if they passed by him. Lennox says they didn't.

Macbeth says the air they ride upon is infected, and he damns everyone who trusts them. (Ironically, he trusts himself.) He could swear he heard the galloping of horses. He asks Lennox who has come.

Lennox says its two or three men reporting that Macduff has fled to England. Macbeth can hardly believe his ears, so Lennox has to reconfirm the news.

Macbeth thinks his plans had been anticipated. He complains that if you don't do something immediately when you think of it, you might not get a chance to do it. He now promises to act on impulse. The next thing he wants to do is raid Macduff's castle, seize the town of Fife, kill Macduff's wife and his children and anyone else who could inherit Macduff's wealth. He swears he will do this before he cools down. He's had enough of apparitions, he wants to meet the messengers. He tells Lennox to bring them to him. Then they go.

Act 4 Scene 2

Lady Macduff, her son and Ross enter. She asks Ross why her husband has left Scotland.

Ross tells her to be patient, but she replies that her husband had no patience. She thinks he was mad to run away. She's say that even if you're not a traitor, fear can make you look like one.

Ross says it's hard to tell whether it was wisdom or fear that made Macduff run to England. But Lady Macduff can't believe it's wisdom to leave his wife and children and his house and titles in an unsafe place. She concludes that he doesn't love his family as he has no instinct to look after them. She mentions how the smallest of birds will fight against the owl, if it threatens its young. She says her husband is fearful, which is why he's run away. She can see no wisdom in it.

Ross tells her to compose herself. He reiterates that her husband is noble, wise and judicious. He says it's not safe for him to say too much, but times are bad if nearly everybody is being accused of being a traitor. He likens it to being tossed around in an ocean and getting nowhere. He says he will leave now but will come back shortly. He says when things are bad it will either stop or improve back to the way it was. He then blesses Lady Macduff.

Lady Macduff says her child is now fatherless. Ross says he has to go before he starts crying. Then he leaves.

Lady Macduff tells her son that his father's dead. She asks him how he's going to live now.

The son replies that he will live like a bird. She asks him if he means eating worms and flies. He says he means he will live on whatever he can. She says he would easily be trapped as he doesn't understand fear. (That's ironic, as she has accused her husband of being too fearful. Perhaps Macduff has more of the survival instinct in him than his son, who says hunters won't want him.) The son also says his father is not dead, no matter what she says.

Lady Macduff insists that her husband is dead. She asks her son what he would do without a father. The son says what should she do without a husband. She says she could buy twenty. He says she would only sell them again. Lady Macduff commends his wit.

The son asks his mother if his father is a traitor. Lady Macduff says he is. Then the son asks for a definition of the word. She says it's someone who makes a promise and breaks it. He asked her if that applies to everyone. She says it does and all traitors should all be hanged. He wants to know who should hang them, and his mother replies 'honest men'. He can't understand how the honest men can hang the dishonest men, as there are far more of the latter in this world. She laughs at his joke, but then repeats her question about what he would do without a father.

The boy says he cannot be dead, as otherwise his mother would be crying. The fact that she is not crying is a good sign that he will have a new father soon. She calls him a silly chatterbox.

Then a messenger enters. He tells Lady Macduff that something terribly dangerous is coming. He tells not to be there when it arrives. Then he goes as he fears for his own safety.

Lady Macduff asks where she should go. She says she's done nothing wrong. But she says it's quite womanly to say that.

Then the murderers enter and she asks them who they are. The first murderer asks her where her husband is. She says she hopes he is not anywhere where they can find him. The first murderer calls Macduff a traitor, to which the son says it's a lie. The first murderer stabs the son. He says he has been killed and urges his mother to run away. She runs offstage screaming 'murder!' but is pursued by the murderers, while her son dies onstage.

Act 4 Scene 3

Malcolm and Macduff enter, with the former saying they should find a shady place where they can sit down and cry.

Macduff says they should defend their homeland with their swords. Each day there are new widows, orphans and sorrows. Scotland is crying out in pain.

Malcolm says he will fix all of this when the time is right. He says he can't even speak the name of the tyrant, especially as Macbeth was once considered to be honest. He thinks Macduff is a favourite of Macbeth as he is uninjured so far. For all Malcolm knows, Macbeth could have sent Macduff south to trap him.

Macduff simply says that he's not treacherous. To that, Malcolm replies that Macbeth is, though. He adds that even a virtuous person will do what his king tells him to. Even the brightest angel in heaven, Lucifer, fell from grace.

Macduff says he's lost hope in convincing Malcolm to fight on his side against Macbeth. Malcolm says the hope was lost in his doubts about him. He asks him why he left his wife and child behind. He tells him not to misinterpret his suspicions and to just give honest answers.

Macduff says the country is bleeding because of the tyrant. He says he cannot be corrupted by Macbeth, not for all the riches in the world.

Malcolm tells Macduff not to be offended. He agrees that Scotland is sinking under Macbeth's rule and that the country is crying and bleeding. He thinks he could raise an army, as the English have promised him thousands of troops. But even if he can end Macbeth's rule, how can he be sure the country will be better off than before? Perhaps it will suffer a worse fate, once a new king is in place.

Macduff can't understand what he means exactly, so Malcolm explains that he is talking about himself. He says Macbeth will seem as pure as snow in comparison.

Macduff says no one is worse than Macbeth. To that, Malcolm admits that Macbeth is murderous and evil in so many ways. But Malcolm says his sexual desires are such that no woman would be safe in Scotland if he were king. Therefore, it would be better for Macbeth to rule.

Macduff replies that endless greed and lust is a kind of tyranny in itself, which has caused the downfall of many kings. But the throne belongs to Malcolm. He should find a way to satisfy his desires in secret, while appearing virtuous on the surface. There are plenty of women for a king if he wants them.

Malcolm says he is also greedy. He will take land, jewels and houses from Scotland's nobles. He would invent false quarrels, if he had to, just to gather more wealth.

Macduff says greed is worse than lust, as he will never grow out of it. However, Scotland has enough treasure to satisfy him, if he becomes king. Anyway, Malcolm must have good sides to his character.

Malcolm says he doesn't have a good side. He says he lacks all the qualities that a king needs. All he has is vices.

Macduff calls out the name of his country in frustration. Malcolm says if Macduff thinks he's fit to be king he should let him know.

Macduff says he must be joking, as he's not fit to live, let alone be king. Although his father Duncan was virtuous, it seems as if Malcolm is anything but. Malcolm's mother was always praying, but all for nothing. Scotland's hope is dead, according to Macduff.

Then Malcolm says the passionate outburst has proved Macduff's integrity. Suddenly, Malcolm has no doubt that Macduff is trustworthy. He says he can't believe people because Macbeth has tried many times to trick him. Now, Malcolm says he will be guided by Macduff. He says he hasn't done any of the bad things that he claimed to have done earlier in the scene. These are the first lies he's ever told and now he is ready to serve his country. He adds that before Macduff arrived, old Siward agreed to commit 10,000 soldiers for battle. Now they can join forces and increase their chances of success. He asks Macduff why he is so quiet.

Macduff says it's hard to make sense of two very different stories.

At this point, a doctor enters. Malcolm tells Macduff they'll speak more later and then he asks the doctor if King Edward is coming.

The doctor says King Edward is coming to offer cures to a bunch of sick people, who can be healed by him simply touching them. Malcolm thanks the doctor, who then leaves.

Macduff asked what kind of disease he is talking about, to which Malcolm replies 'evil'. Malcolm says he's seen Edward's miraculous powers of healing many times during his stay in England. This power will be inherited by his descendants. As well as that, Edward can prophesy the future. He is favoured by God.

Then Ross enters, and Macduff wonders who's coming. Malcolm says his clothes indicate that he is a Scotsman.

Macduff welcomes the stranger, and Malcolm says he recognises him now. He says that they have been kept apart by circumstances and hopes that will change. Ross says he hopes so too.

Macduff asks Ross if Scotland is in the same situation. Ross replies that the country's too afraid to even look at itself. It's not the place they were born in, but it is the place still to die in.

Macduff says the report is poetic, yet it sounds true. Malcolm asks about the recent news, to which Ross replies that awful things happen every minute.

Macduff asks about his wife, but Ross says she is well, as are his children. He says at least they were when he left them. Macduff asks Ross to expand on that, so he says he heard rumours that good men are ready to rebel against Macbeth. Even women would fight if Malcolm and Macduff join the rebellion.

Malcolm tells Ross that he is returning to Scotland with Lord Siward, a very experienced Christian soldier, and 10,000 troops.

Ross wishes he had some good news to respond with. Instead he has the kind of news that should be 'howled out in the desert air' where no one can hear it.

Macduff wants to know exactly what it's about. Does it affect everyone or just one of them?

Ross says no decent person can be immune from sorrow, but the main part of the bad news affects Macduff.

To that, Macduff responds by saying he would like to know immediately. Ross warns Macduff that this news will be the worst he's ever heard. Macduff says he thinks he can guess what that is. Then Ross reveals that Macduff's castle was attacked and his wife and children savagely slaughtered. He is afraid to reveal more details in case it results in the death of Macduff.

Malcolm shouts to the heavens and then to Macduff, telling him not to keep his grief to himself. Malcolm tells Macduff to put his grief into words, otherwise it will be too much to bear for his heart.

Macduff asks if his children were killed too. To this, Ross replies that Macduff's wife, his children, his servants and everyone else who could be found, were murdered.

Macduff complains that he was away when it happened. He asks again if his wife was killed too. Ross replies that he's already said that she was.

Malcolm tells Macduff to be comforted by the thought of revenge on Macbeth. However, Macduff says Macbeth doesn't have children. He asks again if all his pretty children and his wife died in one fell swoop.

Malcolm urges him to fight like a man, but Macduff says he has to feel it like a man first. He feels very sorry because his family didn't do anything wrong. He hopes they can rest in peace.

Malcolm tells Macduff to let anger sharpen his sword. Grief can be converted into anger.

Macduff says he could go on crying like a woman and bragging about revenge, but he doesn't want to wait to get it. He wants to be face-to-face with Macbeth.

Malcolm says that Macduff now sounds like a man. He says they should go and see King Edward as the army is now ready and Macbeth is ripe for the picking. Then they all go.

Act 5 Scene 1

A doctor and a waiting-gentlewoman enter.

The doctor says he has stayed up late but so far hasn't seen any evidence of Lady Macbeth's sleepwalking.

The gentleman replies that since Macbeth went to war, Lady Macbeth has got out of bed, written something down while staying asleep and then returned to bed.

The doctor says it's unnatural to act as if you are awake when you're asleep. He asks if Lady Macbeth's said anything. To that, the gentleman says she will not repeat it.

The doctor says he needs to know, but the gentlewoman says she will not tell anyone, as no one else witnessed it.

Lady Macbeth enters, holding a candle, and the gentlewoman says she's coming. The doctor asks how she got the candle. The gentlewoman replies that it's by her bedside.

The doctor says Lady Macbeth's eyes are open, but the gentlewoman reminds him that she can't see anything. He asks her what she's doing now. She tells him Lady Macbeth is washing her hands.

Lady Macbeth speaks saying there's still a spot of blood on her hands. The doctor hears this and says he is going to write down what she says to help him remember better.

Lady Macbeth rubs hands together and talks to an imaginary spot of blood. She commands it to leave. She mentions the mist or fog that awaits her in hell. It seems as if she is talking to her husband, as she addresses the air saying that it's nonsense. She can't understand why this imaginary person, who is a soldier, is afraid. She says they don't need to be scared, as their guilt cannot be proven. However, she is dismayed by the amount of blood that the old man had in him.

The doctor asks the gentlewoman if she heard that. Lady Macbeth continues her ranting and raving, by asking, in doggerel verse, what happened to the Thane of Fife's wife. (Of course, she's talking about Lady Macduff.) She wonders if her hands will ever be clean. She then talks to an imaginary person (probably her husband), telling it to stop what it's doing and stop acting startled, as that will ruin everything.

The doctor tells the gentlewoman to go, as she's heard things that she shouldn't have.

The gentlewoman says that Lady Macbeth has said something she shouldn't have, and she's sure of that.

Lady Macbeth continues by saying she still has the smell of blood on her little hand. Even all the perfume of Arabia couldn't make it smell better. Then she sighs.

The doctor remarks on how she sighs, and thinks she is carrying a heavy burden on her heart. The gentlewoman says she wouldn't want a heart like that even if she were queen. After some wordplay, the doctor says he cannot treat Lady Macbeth, as her mental illness is beyond his medical knowledge. He says he knows sleepwalkers who have died without any guilt to worry about.

Lady Macbeth continues by telling herself to wash her hands and put on her nightgown. It's almost as if she is outside of herself, as she addresses herself in the second person. She tells herself not to look pale (echoing what she told her husband during the banquet scene). She tells herself that Banquo is buried and he cannot return.

The doctor asks if this is true.

Lady Macbeth continues telling herself to go to bed. She says she hears a knocking at the gate. She tells herself to hold hands and not worry about what has been done, for it cannot be undone. Then she tells herself to go to bed before exiting.

The doctor asks if she will go to bed now, to which the gentlewoman says she will immediately. The doctor continues by saying there are evil rumours everywhere. Unnatural things can cause the supernatural to happen, he says. Guilty people will confess in their sleep. He adds that Lady Macbeth needs a priest more than a doctor. He tells the gentlewoman to look after Lady Macbeth and remove anything that she might injure herself with. He tells her to keep constant watch on Lady Macbeth before wishing the gentlewoman good night. He says he has some strong opinions but doesn't want to voice them.

The gentlewoman wishes him good night and they both exit.

Act 5 Scene 2

We hear drums and we see flags. Menteith, Caithness, Angus, Lennox and soldiers enter with a Drummer.

Menteith says the English army is near. It is being led by Malcolm, his uncle Siward and Macduff. He says they are motivated by revenge. That motivation is so strong it would even make dead men come alive.

Angus says they will meet at Birnam Wood, as that is the route they taking.

Caithness wants to know if Donalbain will be with his brother, Malcolm. Lennox replies that Donalbain is definitely not there. However, Siward's son will be one of the un-bearded men fighting in this battle, hoping to become fully fledged men. (Interestingly, the witches have more of a beard than some of the soldiers!)

Menteith asks what Macbeth is doing, to which Caithness replies that Macbeth is fortifying his castle, making his defence is stronger. We hear that although some say Macbeth's insane, others say he's bravely furious. One thing's for sure, he's completely lost control of himself.

Angus says that Macbeth must feel the blood from the secret murders sticking to his hands. Rebel armies are about to punish him for his breach of trust. The soldiers he commands do not love him. He's like a tiny thief wearing giants robes.

Menteith seems to have some sympathy as he thinks Macbeth is like two people: his senses are acting one way, while the rest of him is in shock about what he has done.

Caithness says they should keep marching on to give their loyalty to somebody who deserves it, like Malcolm. If they shed their own blood, they can help cure the country sickness.

Lennox adds that much-needed blood will be given up to water the royal flower, represented by Malcolm, and kill off the weeds, or Macbeth. He also urges them to march on and they exit marching.

Act 5 Scene 3

Macbeth, the doctor and attendants enter.

Macbeth tells the doctor not to bring him any more reports. He says he doesn't care if everyone deserts him. He says he won't be scared until Birnam Wood moves itself to Dunsinane. He adds that Malcolm was born from a woman and that he was told by the spirits not to fear anyone that was born that way. He asks to be left alone and adds that his mind and heart will not shake with doubt or fear.

A servant enters an Macbeth immediately insults him, by saying he hopes the devil turns his stupid white skin black. Then he asks a servant why he looks like a frightened goose.

The servant replies that there are 10,000, and Macbeth interrupts asking if he means geese. The servant clarifies and says he means soldiers.

Macbeth tells the servant to go and pinch his cheeks to bring some colour back into his face. He calls him cowardly. He says the servant's face may spread fear. He asks him what soldiers, to which the servant replies the English army. Macbeth tells him to leave immediately, which is what he does.

Macbeth calls out to Seyton, a homonym for Satan, and tells him he's sick at heart. He says that the battle will either secure his position for ever or else it will see him lose his throne. He says he's lived long enough, and now he feels like a yellowing leaf in autumn. He says he cannot enjoy the gifts of old age, as all he expects are curses.

Seyton arrives and asks Macbeth what he wants. Macbeth asks him for news. Seyton says all reports have been confirmed. To that, Macbeth says he'll fight on until all the flesh is hacked from his bones. Then he asks for his armour.

Seyton tells him he doesn't need it yet, but Macbeth says he'll put it on anyway. He orders his attendants to send out more cavalry to scour the whole country and hang anyone spreading fear. Once again he asks for his armour. Then he asks the doctor how Lady Macbeth is. (He seems more interested in self-preservation than his wife!)

The doctor says Lady Macbeth is not exactly sick, but she is troubled: she keeps seeing visions that stop her sleeping.

Macbeth tells the doctor to cure her. He asks him whether or not he can treat the diseased mind. He asked the doctor if he can take away memories of sorrow. He suggests using some kind of antidote to raise all the troubling thoughts that are weighing heavily upon her.

The doctor says that can only be done by the patient. Then Macbeth becomes impatient, and says you might as well throw medicine to the dogs. He won't have anything to do with it. Once again he calls for his armour and also for his lance. He tells the doctor to send out the soldiers. He tells the doctor the thanes are running away. He tells the doctor to hurry up. He wonders if the doctor can figure out what's wrong with the country. If he could cure it, Macbeth will applaud him. He then says pull it off. It's difficult to tell whether he means that the armour should be taken off, or whether he means that the doctor should pull off a miracle and cure the country. The latter seems likely as he then asks the doctor what drugs he would use and has he heard of any cures.

The doctor replies that the preparation for war certainly sounds like something he can hear.

Macbeth tells the doctor to bring the armour and follow him. He maintains he will not be afraid to die until Birnam Forest moves to Dunsinane.

At this point, the doctor says he wishes he were far away from Dunsinane. He says money alone would not tempt him back. Then they both exit.

Act 5 Scene 4

We hear drums and we see the colour of the flags before Malcolm, old Siward, young Siward, Macduff, Menteith, Caithness, Angus, Lennox, Ross and soldiers come marching in with a drummer and a flag.

Malcolm says he hopes the time is coming when people will be safe in their bedrooms.

Menteith says he has no doubt that will happen. Siward asks the name of the forest behind them, to which Menteith replies it's Birnam Wood.

Malcolm says they should tell every soldier to break off a branch and hold it in front of him. That way they can camouflage themselves, so Macbeth will have less idea about how many there are of them. The soldiers shout in unison that they will do it.

Siward says they have no news apart from the fact that Macbeth is still in Dunsinane and won't stop them laying siege to the castle.

Malcolm says that Macbeth wants them to lay siege. He adds that a lot of Macbeth soldiers are deserting and they don't have the fight for a battle against Macbeth's enemies.

Macduff says that they shouldn't judge the situation until they achieve their objective.

Siward says blows in battle are more certain than speculation. He suggests that they move forward. So the army exits, marching ahead.

Act 5 Scene 5

Macbeth, Seyton and soldiers enter with a drummer and a flag.

Macbeth commands them to put the flags on the outer walls. He says the castle was so strong they can laugh at the siege. Those laying siege can sit out there until they die of hunger and disease. Had it not been for the huge number of deserters, they could have joined them in battle in front of the castle and beaten back to England.

The cry of women is heard offstage and Macbeth asks what is. Seyton says its women crying, before exiting.

Macbeth says he's almost forgotten what it feels like to be afraid. He says at one time he would have been afraid by shriek in the night and his hair stood up if he heard a ghost story. But now he's had so many horrors to endure, horrible things cannot startle him any longer. At that point, Seyton returns. Macbeth, presumably hears a cry, as he asks Seyton what was the cry for. His doctor reports the Queen is dead.

Macbeth says she would have died later anyway. It was bound to happen. Tomorrow, and tomorrow, and tomorrow. He says the days creep slowly until the end of time. Each day brings a fool closer to his death, when the candle goes out. Life is nothing more than poor actor, who performs on stage for an hour and then disappears forever. It's like a noisy and dramatic story told by an idiot that has no meaning. Then the messenger enters, and Macbeth asks him to tell him the news, quickly.

The messenger says he should say what he saw but he doesn't know how to say it. Macbeth tells him to spit it out.

The messenger says he was standing on the hill, when he thought he saw Birnam Wood move. Macbeth calls him a liar. The messenger says punish me if it's not true. He says again he's seen a moving forest.

Macbeth tells to the messenger, if he's lying he will be hanged from the nearest tree until he dies of hunger. If he's telling the truth, Macbeth doesn't care if the messenger does the same to him. Macbeth speaks to himself saying that his confidence is diminishing. He is beginning to doubt himself. He was told not to worry until Birnam Wood comes to Dunsinane. Now it's happening. They should prepare to fight and go out of the castle. If what the messenger says is true, there's no point running away or staying in the castle. He says he's getting tired of living now, and he would like to see the world plunged into chaos. He says ring the alarm bells, and let the wind blow. At least they can die with their armour on their backs. They all leave.

Act 5 Scene 6

Malcolm, old Siward, Macduff and the Army enter carrying branches, along with a drummer and a flag.

Malcolm says they are close enough now. He tells them to throw their branches on the ground and show the enemy who they really are. He tells his uncle, Siward, and his son, Young Siward, to lead the first charge into battle. Macduff and Malcolm will do the rest, according to their tactics.

Siward wishes them good luck. He says if he meets Macbeth's army, he'd rather lose if they cannot fight.

Macduff orders all the trumpets to be blown to announce the arrival of blood and death. Then they all exit.

Act 5 Scene 7

Trumpets sound and the noise of battle can be heard as Macbeth enters.

Macbeth says he's been tied to a stake and he can't run away. He's like a bear, being attacked for the amusement of others. He asks where is the man who wasn't born naturally from a woman. That's the only man he needs to be afraid of.

Young Siward enters and asks Macbeth his name. Macbeth answers that he'll be frightened when he hears it. Young Siward says he won't be, even if his name was hotter than any in hell. Macbeth reveals his identity. Young Siward says there is no name he hates more. Macbeth says no name is more frightening. Young Siward tells Macbeth that he's a liar and a disgusting tyrant. He'll speak to him with his sword. In the fighting that ensues, Young Siward is killed.

Macbeth speaks to the dead body of young Siward, telling the corpse that he doesn't fear anyone born naturally from a woman: their swords don't frighten him.

Macbeth exits and Macduff enters the scene with trumpet and battle sounds continuing. Macduff says that the noises are coming from over there. He shouts to Macbeth that he should show his face. He says if someone else kills Macbeth, the ghosts of Lady Macduff and his children will forever haunt him. Macduff says he can't be bothered to fight mercenaries, or soldiers who only fight for money. He thinks Macbeth must be in the area where there's a lot of noise, as it sounds like there's an announcement going on. He only asks for the luck to find Macbeth, and no more than that.

Macduff exits and more battle noises are heard as Malcolm and old Siward enter. Siward says the castle has been surrendered without a fight. Macbeth's soldiers are fighting on both sides, while the Thanes are fighting bravely. The battle has been almost won and it seems like there's not much left to do.

Malcolm says the enemy troops are fighting as if they don't want to hurt them. Siward suggests they go into the castle. As they both exit the scene, the battle noise continues.

Act 5 Scene 8

Macbeth enters and asks why should he commit suicide like an ancient Roman when he would rather see his enemy suffering wounds than himself.

Macduff enters and tells Macbeth to turn around, calling him a dog. Macbeth says to Macduff that he's the only man he has avoided. Macbeth says he feels guilty for killing all of Macduff's family, so he should leave.

Macduff says he has nothing to say and his sword will do the talking. He says there are no words to describe how evil Macbeth is. Then they fight.

Macbeth says to Macduff that he's wasting his time trying to wound him. He might as well stab the air. Macbeth says that he lives a charmed life and he cannot be harmed by anyone naturally born from a woman.

Macduff tells Macbeth to forget about his charm. The evil spirit should have told Macbeth that Macduff is not naturally born. He tells Macbeth that he was a Caesarean-section birth.

Macbeth curses Macduff for telling him. He says his courage has melted away, but he doesn't believe that evil witches anymore. They tricked him with double meanings, raising his hopes before destroying them. He says he won't fight with Macduff.

Then Macduff says that Macbeth should surrender. He says they'll put him in a freak show with unusual monsters.

Macbeth says he's not going to surrender and kiss the ground in front of Malcolm's feet. He won't suffer the humiliation of being taunted by common people. He will fight to the end and will put up his shield. He tells Macduff to try to kill him if he dares. He adds that the first man to stop fighting will be damned forever. They exit the stage still fighting. Trumpets and battle noises continue. They re-enter fighting and then Macbeth is slain. One army's trumpet sounds the call to retreat while the other sounds the call of victory. Malcolm, Siward, Ross, the thanes and the soldiers all enter with a drummer and a flag.

Malcolm says she wishes all his friends could have survived this battle.

Siward replies that in every battle some people will be casualties. He says judging by the lack of dead men that he can see, the victory didn't cost very much in terms of lives.

Malcolm says that Macduff is still missing, as is young Siward.

Ross says that young Siward has paid the soldier's price, which is death. Sadly, Young Siward lived long only just enough to become a man and, as soon as he proved his manhood by fighting, he died.

Siward asks for confirmation of his son's death. To that, Ross says young Siward has been carried off. Ross adds that if the grief were equal to what young Siward is worth, the sorrow would be never ending.

Checking for potential cowardice, Siward asks whether the wounds were on his front, to which Ross replies they were. Of course, Siward would be mortified to hear otherwise, as it would indicate Young Siward was killed as he retreated. Instead, wounds on the front suggest bravery. Siward has rightly assumed that his son faced the foe and fought valiantly.

Siward describes his son as God's soldier now. He says no son could have died more honourably.

Malcolm says that young Siward is worth more sorrow and he will mourn for his death.

Siward says he is not worth more than that. His son died well, and paid his dues. He hopes God is now with his son. He says it looks like better news is coming.

At that, Macduff enters carrying Macbeth's head.

Macduff greets Malcolm as king, as that is what he is now. He says he has Macbeth's head and now they are free from his tyranny. He says all the Lords of Scotland want the same thing and they want to pronounce Malcolm as king of Scotland. In unison, they all chant: 'Hail, King of Scotland!' Then trumpets herald the new king.

Malcolm says it won't be long before he rewards everyone who deserves reward. He renames all of his thanes, calling them earls. They are the first earls in Scotland's history. He adds that much needs to be done in this new era. All of their exiled friends must return home and justice must be done to all those killed in the name of Macbeth and his queen, who is rumoured to have committed suicide. He says they will do all of these things at the right time in the right place and in the name of God. He thanks them all and invites them to his coronation at Scone. The trumpets play and they all exit.

Useful information/Glossary

Allegory: extended metaphor, like the grim reaper representing death, e.g. Scrooge symbolizing capitalism.

Alliteration: same consonant sound repeating, e.g. 'She sells sea shells'.

Allusion: reference to another text/person/place/event.

Ascending tricolon: sentence with three parts, each increasing in power, e.g. 'ringing, drumming, shouting'.

Aside: character speaking so some characters cannot hear what is being said. Sometimes, an aside is directly to the audience. It's a dramatic technique which reveals the character's inner thoughts and feelings.

Assonance: same vowel sounds repeating, e.g. 'Oh no, won't Joe go?'

Bathos: abrupt change from sublime to ridiculous for humorous effect.

Blank verse: lines of unrhymed iambic pentameter.

Compressed time: when the narrative is fast-forwarding through the action.

Descending tricolon: sentence with three parts, each decreasing in power, e.g. 'shouting, talking, whispering'.

Denouement: tying up loose ends, the resolution.

Diction: choice of words or vocabulary.

Dilated time: opposite compressed time, here the narrative is in slow motion.

Direct address: second person narrative, predominantly using the personal pronoun 'you'.

Dramatic action verb: manifests itself in physical action, e.g. I punched him in the face.

Dramatic irony: audience knows something that the character is unaware of.

Ellipsis: leaving out part of the story and allowing the reader to fill in the narrative gap.

Epistolary: letter or correspondence-driven narrative.

Flashback/Analepsis: going back in time to the past, interrupting the chronological sequence.

Flashforward/Prolepsis: going forward in time to the future, interrupting the chronological sequence.

Foreshadowing/Adumbrating: suggestion of plot developments that will occur later in the narrative.

Gothic: another strand of Romanticism, typically with a wild setting, a sensitive heroine, an older man with a 'piercing gaze', discontinuous structure, doppelgangers, guilt and the 'unspeakable' (according to Eve Kosofsky Sedgwick).

Hamartia: character flaw, leading to that character's downfall.

Hyperbole: exaggeration for effect.

Iambic pentameter: a line of ten syllables beginning with a lighter stress alternating with a heavier stress in its perfect form, which sounds like a heartbeat. The stress falls on the even syllables, numbers: 2, 4, 6, 8 and 10, e.g. 'When now I think you can behold such sights'.

Intertextuality: links to other literary texts.

Irony: amusing or cruel reversal of expected outcome or words meaning the opposite to their literal meaning.

Metafiction/Romantic irony: self-conscious exposure of the devices used to create 'the truth' within a work of fiction.

Motif: recurring image use of language or idea that connects the narrative together and creates a theme or mood, e.g. 'green light' in *The Great Gatsby*.

Oxymoron: contradictory terms combined, e.g. deafening silence.

Pastiche: imitation of another's work.

Pathetic fallacy: a form of personification whereby inanimate objects show human attributes, e.g. 'the sea smiled benignly'. The originator of the term, John Ruskin in 1856, used 'the cruel, crawling foam', from Kingsley's *The Sands of Dee*, as an example to clarify what he meant by the 'morbid' nature of pathetic fallacy.

Personification: concrete or abstract object made human, often simply achieved by using a capital letter or a personal pronoun, e.g. 'Nature', or describing a ship as 'she'.

Pun/Double entendre: a word with a double meaning, usually employed in witty wordplay but not always.

Retrospective: account of events after they have occurred.

Romanticism: genre celebrating the power of imagination, spriritualism and nature.

Semantic/lexical field: related words about a single concept, e.g. king, queen and prince are all concerned with royalty.

Soliloquy: character thinks aloud, but is not heard by other characters (unlike in a monologue) giving the audience access to inner thoughts and feelings.

Style: choice of language, form and structure, and effects produced.

Synecdoche: one part of something referring to the whole, e.g. Carker's teeth represent him in *Dombey and Son*.

Syntax: the way words and sentences are placed together.

Tetracolon climax: sentence with four parts, culminating with the last part, e.g. 'I have nothing to offer but blood, toil, tears, and sweat ' (Winston Churchill).

ABOUT THE AUTHOR

Joe Broadfoot Jr is a soccer journalist, who also writes fiction and literary criticism. His former experiences as a DJ took him to far-flung places such as Tokyo, Kobe, Beijing, Hong Kong, Jakarta, Cairo, Dubai, Cannes, Oslo, Bergen and Bodo. He is now a CELTA-qualified English teacher with a first-class honours degree in Literature and an MA in Victorian Studies.

15784343R00062

Printed in Poland
by Amazon Fulfillment
Poland Sp. z o.o., Wrocław